Beginners' Indonesian

Safitri Widagdo

Teach Yourself®

Beginners' Indonesian

Safitri Widagdo

First published in Great Britain in 2016 as *Get Started in Indonesian* by Hodder and Stoughton. An Hachette UK company.

This edition published by Teach Yourself in 2025
An imprint of John Murray Press

This paperback edition published in 2025

1

Editorial support from Haremi Ltd

A CIP catalogue record for this title is available from the British Library

Paperback ISBN 9781399824422
ebook ISBN 9781399824439

Typeset by Integra Software Services Pvt. Ltd., Pondicherry, India

Printed and bound in Great Britain by Clays Ltd, Elcograf S.p.A.

John Murray Press policy is to use papers that are natural, renewable and recyclable products and made from wood grown in sustainable forests. The logging and manufacturing processes are expected to conform to the environmental regulations of the country of origin.

John Murray Press
Carmelite House
50 Victoria Embankment
London EC4Y 0DZ

Nicholas Brealey Publishing
Hachette Book Group
Market Place, Center 53, State Street
Boston, MA 02109, USA

www.teachyourself.com

John Murray Press, part of Hodder & Stoughton Limited
An Hachette UK company

The authorized representative in the EEA is Hachette Ireland, 8 Castlecourt Centre, Castleknock Road, Castleknock, Dublin 15, D15 YF6A, Ireland

Contents

Acknowledgements

The author wishes to warmly thank all those who made this book possible, in particular Emma Green, Priya Das, Cecilia Bembibre and the team at Hodder & Stoughton, Sarah Jane Lewis, Dr Ben Murtagh, Om Jim Sneddon, Ardita Caesari, the SOAS School of Languages, Cultures and Linguistics, and for their support and company, Capability and Jim. This book is dedicated to her family.

About the author

Safitri Widagdo was born in Jakarta, Indonesia, and grew up with one foot in an Indonesian household and the other in the expatriate community. She has taught Indonesian language courses and translation seminars to adult learners and university students at SOAS, University of London. A writer and literary translator, she has a degree in South East Asian Studies from SOAS and a degree in English Literature from the University of Chicago.

About the course

This book consists of an introductory **Pronunciation guide** to familiarize you with the basic sounds of Indonesian and an introduction to **Useful expressions** to help you get the most practical phrases under your belt before you start. The core of the book are 10 units which will help you learn basic language function and introduce key topics for everyday communication.

A little goes a long way! Try to use the book little and often, rather than for long stretches at a time. This will help you to create a study habit, much in the same way you would for a sport or music. Leave the book somewhere handy so that you can pick it up for just a few minutes.

Before you start, make a plan! Setting goals affects the programming of your brain, strengthening neural pathways and ultimately making it more likely that you will achieve those goals. Before you begin, think about how much time you want to devote to learning, which skills or areas you want to focus on, and identify specific ideas you want to be able to communicate or activities you want to engage in.

Track your progress! Start a notebook to use for study, where you can create vocabulary lists, a grammar summary, questions you'd like answered, etc. Keep track of your resources – movies, podcasts, songs or blogs you like – and jot down a few words or expressions you may have recognized or learned. The more you can reflect on your learning process, the deeper your connection with the language will be. For guidance in this process, we recommend Teach Yourself's *Fluentish: Language Learning Planner & Journal*, published by Jo Franco.

Use the tools at the beginning of each unit to help you set goals, plan your time, and keep track of the work you do.

IN THIS UNIT, YOU WILL LEARN HOW TO

Each unit begins with an overview of the language you will be learning and skills you will be acquiring.

MY PROGRESS TRACKER

Use the progress tracker to plan your study time and to keep a record of what you've accomplished. The first column tracks time, and the remaining five columns represent the skills you'll be working on: listening, pronunciation, reading, writing, and spoken interaction.

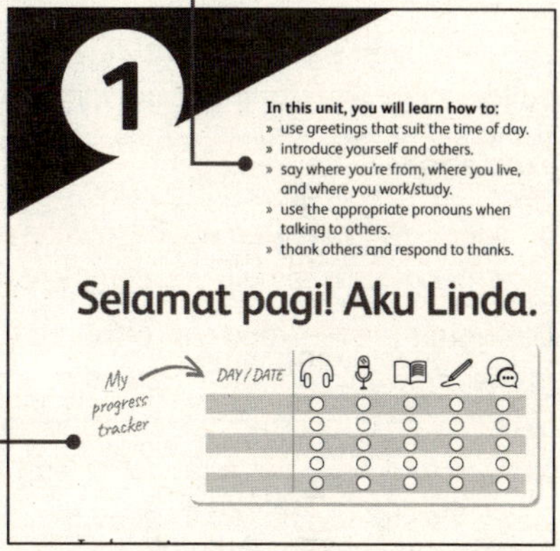

Personalize the tracker: Instead of the date or day, you can enter an increment of time. Add columns for culture, vocabulary, grammar or any other area you wish to focus on. Give yourself a star when you feel you've done particularly well. Make it your own! Review your tracker regularly and see which areas could use more practice.

Use the **Self check** at the end of each unit to evaluate your progress.

Try to practice each skill every day.

The icons in the progress tracker are used throughout the book to help you easily identify and locate the skills you want to practice:

Listening skills

Speaking – pronunciation skills

Reading skills

Writing skills

Speaking – conversation skills

Remember: there are many ways to build your skills in addition to those provided in this book: use a language-learning app, listen to music or podcasts, watch TV shows or movies, go to a restaurant, follow Indonesian social media accounts (there are wonderful teachers who post regularly), read blogs, newspapers or magazines, switch the language settings in your apps to Indonesian, or sign up for a language exchange or a tutor.

Units 1–10

The units open with a **cultural reading** in English and a **Vocabulary builder** page with thematic groupings of related words that can be studied together, as well as **new expressions** – specific words and expressions needed to understand the upcoming conversations or reading passages. You will often notice missing words in the Vocabulary builder. Look for patterns to help you complete the lists.

Dialogues are recorded conversations that you can listen to and practice, beginning with a narrative that helps you understand what you are going to hear, with a focusing question and follow-up activities. It is important to listen to or read this material at least twice; work out the meaning for yourself as far as you can, but use the lists of key words and phrases to help you. As in any conversation, listen for the meaning and don't worry about understanding each individual word. This will come with time. The **Indonesian–English Glossary** at the back of the book allow you to quickly access all the vocabulary that is presented in the course.

The **Language discovery** asks you to think about one or more aspects of the grammar seen in the Conversation. (See below for more information about the learning approach known as the Discovery method.) There are notes throughout to help guide you and draw your attention to interesting language or culture points.

The **Practice** sections give you the opportunity to try out the language that has been presented in the unit; each exercise focuses on listening, reading, writing or speaking. Finally, in every unit there is a short test – **Test yourself** – which enables you to check whether you can now do some of the language tasks covered by that unit. There are also three **Reviews**, after Units 3, 6 and 10, to help you consolidate what you've learned. You can check all your answers in the **Answer key** at the back of the book.

Revise each unit until you can do it without errors before you go on to the next unit. It is important to go back over material in areas where you are making errors, rather than carrying on regardless, which is bound to get you into trouble later.

How to be a successful language learner

The Discovery method

There are lots of philosophies and approaches to language learning, some practical, some quite unconventional, and far too many to list here. Perhaps you know of a few, or even have some techniques of your own. In this book we have incorporated the Discovery method of learning, a sort of DIY approach to language learning. What this means is that you will be encouraged throughout the course to engage your mind and figure out the language for yourself, through identifying patterns, understanding grammar concepts, noticing words that are similar to English, and more.

Simply put, if you figure something out for yourself, you're more likely to understand it. And when you use what you've learned, you're more likely to remember it. And because many of the essential but (let's admit it!) dull details, such as grammar rules, are introduced through the Discovery method, you'll have more fun while learning. Soon, the language will start to make sense and you'll be relying on your own intuition to construct original sentences independently, not just listening and repeating.

Everyone can succeed in learning a language – the key is to know how to learn it.

Learn to learn

There are many strategies that can help you become a successful language learner. Different people have different learning styles and some of these approaches will be more effective for you than others. Use this list as a point of inspiration when you want to find the most effective ways to advance your skills and begin your journey to fluency.

VOCABULARY

Words are the building blocks of language. The more you use the words you're introduced to, the more quickly they'll lodge into your memory. These study tips will help you remember better:

- Say the words out loud as you read them. Listen to the audio several times.
- Write the words over and over again. Create flash cards, drawings and mind maps.
- It helps to group new words in categories, like food or furniture, or according to the situations in which they occur, e.g. restaurant, hotel, sight-seeing, or their functions, e.g. greetings, parting, thanks, apologizing.
- Cover up the English side of the vocabulary list and see if you remember the meaning of the word. Then cover up the Indonesian side, and see if you can remember the word itself.
- Post sticky notes for words for objects around your house.
- Experiment with words. Look for patterns in words, for example, translate words based on how the word *reservation* appears in Indonesian as the word **reservasi**.

GRAMMAR

Grammar gives your language structure. It allows you to experiment with the vocabulary you learn because you'll understand how they work together to create meaning. In other words, you'll begin to develop a feel for the language. Here are some tips to help you study more effectively:

- Write your own grammar glossary and add new information and examples as you go along.
- Experiment with grammar rules. Use old vocabulary to practice new grammar structures.
- Try to find examples of grammar in conversations or other articles.
- When you learn a new verb form, review other verbs you know that follow the same pattern.
- Compare Indonesian structures with your own language or other languages you may already speak. Try to find out some rules on your own and be ready to spot the exceptions.

PRONUNCIATION

The best way to improve your pronunciation is simply to practice as much as possible. Study individual sounds first, then full words and sentences. Don't forget, it's not just about pronouncing letters and words correctly, but using the right intonation. So, when practicing words and sentences, mimic the rising and falling intonation of Indonesian speakers.

- Repeat all of the conversations, line by line. Listen to yourself and try to mimic what you hear.
- Record yourself and compare yourself to the recordings.
- Make a list of words that give you trouble and practice them.

LISTENING AND READING

The conversations in this book include questions to help guide you in your understanding. But you can go further by following some of these tips.

- Imagine the situation. Try to imagine where the scene is taking place and who the main characters are. Let your experience of the world help you guess the meaning of the conversation, e.g. if a conversation takes place in a café, you can predict the kind of vocabulary that will be used.
- Concentrate on the main part. When watching a film in another language you usually get the meaning of the whole story from a few individual shots. Understanding a conversation or text in another language is similar. Concentrate on the main message and don't worry about individual words.
- Learn to cope with uncertainty – don't over-use your dictionary! You don't have to look up every word you don't know – try to deduce the meaning from context. Concentrate on trying to get the gist of the passage and underline the words you don't understand. If after the third time there are still words which prevent you from getting the general meaning of the passage, look them up in the dictionary.

WRITING

You'll have plenty of writing practice using this book. Creating vocabulary lists, grammar summaries and taking good notes as you study is another great opportunity to practice writing.

If you're keeping your lists or notes on your smartphone, computer or tablet, remember to switch the keyboard language to be able to include all accents and special characters. Here are some other ways to practice writing:

- Write out the answers to all Practice and Test Yourself questions.
- Create your own vocabulary lists and a grammar summary.
- Look up writing prompts for language learning or try writing a daily gratitude journal in Indonesian.
- Write out your To Do and shopping lists in Indonesian.
- Join online forums and discussion groups about or in Indonesian.

SPEAKING

The greatest obstacle to speaking a new language is the fear of making a mistake. Keep in mind that you make mistakes in your own language – it's simply part of the human condition. Accept it. Most errors are not serious and they will not affect the meaning. So concentrate on getting your message across and use the mistakes as learning opportunities. Here are some useful tips to help you practice speaking Indonesian:

- Rehearse in Indonesian. Hold a conversation with yourself, using the conversations of the units as models and the structures you have learned previously.
- When you're going about your day, e.g. buying groceries, ordering food and drinks, do it in Indonesian in your mind! Look at objects around you and try to name them in Indonesian. Look at people around you and try to describe them in detail.
- Answer all of the questions in the book out loud. Say the dialogues out loud, then try to replace sentences with ones that are true for you. Try to role-play different situations in the book.
- Keep talking. The best way to improve your fluency in a language is to talk every time you have the opportunity to do so: keep the conversations flowing and don't worry about the mistakes. If you get stuck for a particular word, don't let the conversation stop; simplify what you want to say; paraphrase or replace the unknown word with one you do know.

Learning a language takes work. But the work can be a lot of fun! So, let's begin!

Selamat belajar!

Enjoy learning Indonesian!

Pronunciation guide

You'll be glad to know that with some exceptions, Indonesian pronunciation is very straightforward. The language also shares many sounds with English, even if some are spelled differently, and contains only one ambiguous sound: **e**.

Vowels

00.01

a	**lima**	*five*	the 'a' in car with the mouth open wider
i	**tiga**	*three*	the 'ee' in leech or the 'i' in chin
u	**buku**	*book*	the 'oo' in book
e	**empat**	*four*	a schwa or the 'e' in father
é	**pena**	*pen*	the 'e' in bet
o	**orang**	*person*	the 'o' in lot or the 'ou' in bought
aa	**maaf**	*sorry*	pronounced as two separate 'a' sounds
ai	**pantai**	*beach*	the vowel sound in bye
au	**danau**	*lake*	the vowel sound in wow
oi	**letoi**	*tired*	the vowel sound in toy

Children in Indonesia learn the sequence of vowels as a, i, u, e, o. You can use this sequence to prompt you to think of vowels as they are pronounced in the Indonesian way.

The letter **e** can be pronounced as **e** or **é** in Indonesian. The old spelling showed the difference, but the current spelling does not distinguish between them. When you're not sure about how to pronounce a word, you can say it as if you are asking a question and receive feedback from the person you're speaking to.

Consonants

00.02

Consonants pronounced as in English

b	**bayi**	*baby*
d	**dua**	*two*
g	**gang**	*alley*
h	**hari**	*day*
j	**jalan**	*street*
m	**mata**	*eye*
n	**nama**	*name*
ng	**ngeri**	*scary*
s	**salah**	*wrong*
w	**wajan**	*wok*
y	**ya**	*yes*

Consonants with a difference

c	**cepat**	*quick*	the 'ch' in chop
f	**feri**	*ferry*	like the English 'f' but sometimes as 'p'
k	**kota**	*city*	like the English 'k' but without aspiration
kh	**khas**	*typical*	the 'ch' in loch but sometimes as 'k'
l	**lagi**	*more*	the light English 'l' such as the 'l' in like
ny	**nyala**	*ablaze*	the 'ny' in onion
p	**pas**	*exact*	like the English 'p' but without aspiration
r	**roti**	*bread*	the rolling or rolled 'r'
sy	**syal**	*shawl*	pronounced as spelled or as 'sh'
t	**toko**	*store*	like the English 't' but without aspiration
v	**vespa**	*scooter*	like the English 'f' but sometimes as 'p'

THE OLD SPELLING

Indonesian has undergone several spelling reforms, but the old spelling is still here today in place names, people's names, and iconic name brands. **Soekarno**, for example, is the old spelling of **Sukarno**.

the old spelling		the new spelling		
oe	**lampoe**	u	**lampu**	*lamp*
tj	**tjerita**	c	**cerita**	*story*
dj	**Djakarta**	j	**Jakarta**	*Jakarta*
é	**énak**	e	**enak**	*delicious*
j	**sjair**	y	**syair**	*poem*
nj	**njala**	ny	**nyala**	*ablaze*
sj	**sjukuran**	sy	**syukuran**	*thanksgiving*
ch	**achir**	kh	**akhir**	*end*

Now that a number of older Indonesian texts such as historical documents and martial arts stories have been digitized and can be found on the internet, you can browse through them to find words in which **e** is written and pronounced as **é**.

Stress

00.03

Where the stress falls depends on where you are in Indonesia because of the influence of local languages or dialects. In many cases, the stress falls on the penultimate (second to last) syllable of a word. In a word with only two syllables, that would be the first syllable of the word.

empat perem***pa***tan

Useful expressions

Greetings, partings and courtesies

halo	*hello* (phone greeting)
dah, sampai jumpa	*goodbye*
sampai bertemu lagi	*see you, until we meet again*
sampai besok	*see you tomorrow*
sampai nanti	*see you later*
Apa kabar?	*How are you?*
Kabar baik.	*I'm well.*
Ada apa?	*What's the matter?*
Tidak ada apa-apa.	*Nothing's the matter.*
permisi	*excuse me, pardon me*
silakan	*please, go ahead*
maaf	*sorry*
tidak apa-apa	*it's nothing, no worries*
terima kasih	*thank you*
sama-sama	*likewise, you're welcome*

Making yourself understood

tolong ulang sekali lagi	*please repeat once again*
tolong ulang pelan-pelan	*please repeat slowly*
Apa arti ...?	*What is the meaning of ...?*
saya tidak tahu	*I don't know*
saya tidak mengerti	*I don't understand*

Needing assistance

tolong	*please, help*
saya beralergi..., saya punya alergi...	*I have an allergy to ...*
tolong ambilkan bonnya	*please bring me the check/bill*
numpang tanya..., bisa saya bertanya...	*may I ask ..., can I ask ...*
bisa bicara dengan ...	*may I speak with ...*

Some useful phrases

Selamat tidur!	*Sleep well!*
Selamat makan!	*Enjoy your meal!*
Semoga cepat sembuh!	*Get well soon!*
Selamat ulang tahun!	*Happy birthday!*

Counting

In Indonesian, the basic units for numbers are between zero and nine. Larger numbers come in groups similar to those in English, such as **belasan** (*teens*), **puluhan** (*tens*), and **ratusan** (*hundreds*).

0	nol *or* kosong	10	sepuluh
1	satu	11	sebelas
2	dua	12	dua belas
3	tiga	13	tiga belas
4	empat	14	empat belas
5	lima	15	lima belas
6	enam	16	enam belas
7	tujuh	17	tujuh belas
8	delapan	18	delapan belas
9	sembilan	19	sembilan belas
20	dua puluh	25	dua puluh lima
21	dua puluh satu	26	dua puluh enam
22	dua puluh dua	27	dua puluh tujuh
23	dua puluh tiga	28	dua puluh delapan
24	dua puluh empat	29	dua puluh sembilan
100	seratus	500	lima ratus
1,000	seribu	5,000	lima ribu
10,000	sepuluh ribu	50,000	lima puluh ribu
100,000	seratus ribu	500,000	lima ratus ribu

In Indonesia, being familiar with large numbers is very useful because prices of everyday goods run into the tens and hundreds of thousands. You'll be pleased to know that composing large numbers in Indonesian is done in a similar way to how it is done in English. Start with the largest group, for example the **ribuan** (*thousands*), and move to the second largest, for example the **ratusan** (*hundreds*), then to the tens, and so on.

123,450 = 123,000 + 400 + 50

seratus dua puluh tiga ribu empat ratus lima puluh

one hundred (and) twenty-three thousand, four hundred (and) fifty

1

In this unit, you will learn how to:

» use greetings that suit the time of day.
» introduce yourself and others.
» say where you're from, where you live, and where you work/study.
» use the appropriate pronouns when talking to others.
» thank others and respond to thanks.

Selamat pagi! Aku Linda.

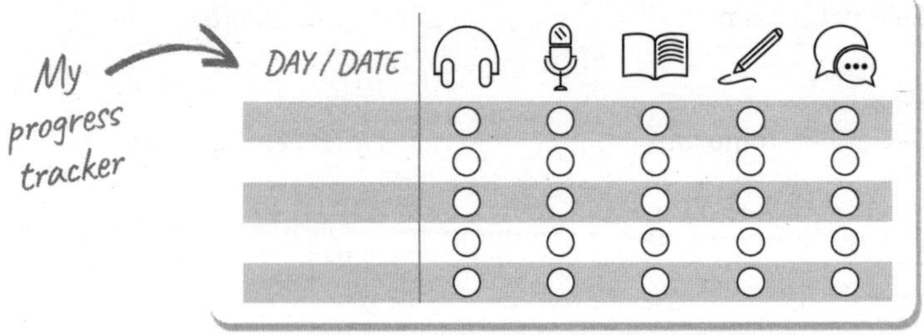

Indonesian

Did you know that for many Indonesians, **bahasa Indonesia** (*Indonesian*) is not their first language either? A person from Indonesia usually belongs to an ethnic group whose language is their **bahasa ibu** (*mother tongue*). Indonesian is learned formally at school as the official language of the republic. It allows people of diverse cultural backgrounds across the archipelagic nation to communicate with one another. The roots of Indonesian lie in classical **bahasa Melayu** (*Malay*), but it is distinct from modern Malay due to the influence of **bahasa Jawa** (*Javanese*). Periods of Dutch and Portuguese colonization also left their mark. Indonesian is a practical language in a region that has welcomed traders and goods from all around the world for many centuries and will continue to do so. It utilizes borrowings from major world languages such as **bahasa Arab** (*Arabic*), **bahasa Cina** (*Chinese*), and **bahasa Inggris** (*English*). You will discover important differences between English and Indonesian, but you will also notice similarities that will help you.

What do these Indonesian words mean?. **Eropa, Jepang, telepon, universitas, akuntan, dokter**

Vocabulary builder

01.01 Look at the words and phrases and complete the English translations. Then listen to the recording and imitate the pronunciation of the speakers.

GREETINGS

Selamat pagi	*Good ______ (dawn to 10 a.m.)*
Selamat siang	*Good day (10 a.m. to 3 p.m.)*
Selamat sore	*Good ______ (3 p.m. to 6 p.m.)*
Selamat malam	*Good ______ (after sunset)* *Goodnight*
Permisi.	*Excuse me/us.*
Sampai bertemu lagi.	*Until (we) meet again.*

FORMAL PRONOUNS

saya	*I, me, my*
Anda	*you, your*

INFORMAL PRONOUNS

aku	*I, me, my*
kamu	*you, your*

In Indonesian, pronouns such as *I*, *you*, etc. become *my*, *your*, etc. depending on where the pronouns are placed. In English, information about a noun such as *doctor* comes before the noun, for example *my doctor*. In Indonesian, it is the reverse: information about the noun comes after it, so that when **saya** is used to mean *my*, it comes after the noun, for example **dokter saya** (*my doctor*).

ESSENTIAL WORDS

siapa	*who*	**apa**	*what*
mana	*where*	**dan**	*and*
ini	*this, these*	**itu**	*that, those*

LOCATION WORDS

dari	*from*
di	*at/in/on*
ke	*to*

NEW EXPRESSIONS

Kenalkan.	*Let me introduce* (lit. *acquaint*) *you.*
Silakan.	*Please./Go ahead.*
nama	*name*
Terima kasih.	*Thank you.*
Sama-sama.	*Likewise./You're welcome.*

Conversation 1

01.02 *Mr Budi (Bapak Budi) runs into his colleague Mrs Wati (Ibu Wati) and Jonathan Curtis.*

1 Where does Jonathan live?

Wati	Selamat sore, Pak Budi.
Budi	Selamat sore, Bu Wati.
Wati	Kenalkan. Ini Jonathan Curtis.
Jon	Panggil saya Jon.
Budi	Saya Budi. Dari mana Anda berasal, Pak Jon?
Jon	Saya berasal dari Liverpool.
Budi	Anda tinggal di mana?
Jon	Saya tinggal di Jakarta.
Budi	Di mana Anda bekerja?
Jon	Saya bekerja di bank. Dan Anda?
Budi	Saya kerja di universitas.
Jon	Nama universitas Anda apa?
Budi	Universitas Palembang. Saya kolega Ibu Wati.
Wati	Permisi, Pak Budi.
Budi	Silakan.
Jon	Sampai bertemu lagi, Pak Budi!
Budi	Sampai bertemu lagi.

panggil	*to call (by name)*
berasal	*come/ originate from*
tinggal	*live, reside*
kerja	*to work*

When you're using **Bapak** and **Ibu** in everyday conversation to mean, respectively, *Mr* and *Ms/Mrs*, they can be abbreviated to **Pak** and **Bu**.

2 Match the Indonesian to the English.

a Anda tinggal di mana?
b Permisi.
c Sampai bertemu lagi.
d Dari mana Anda berasal?

1 *Until we meet again.*
2 *Where do you come from?*
3 *Excuse me.*
4 *Where do you live?*

3 **Read or listen again and answer the questions.**

a Around what time of day do you think it is?

b Where is Pak Jon from?

c Where does Pak Budi work?

d What do you think **kolega** means?

4 01.03 **Now listen to the lines from the conversation and repeat. Be sure to pay attention to the pronunciation.**

Language discovery 1

Find the sentences in the conversation that mean:

a This is Jonathan Curtis. I am Budi.

b Where do you work? I work at a university.

c Where do you come from? Where do you live?

1 GETTING STARTED WITHOUT *IS, AM*, AND *ARE*

In everyday Indonesian, *I am Budi* or *this is Jon* is simply **saya Budi** or **ini Jon**. Similarly, **saya tinggal** is both *I live* and *I am living.*

2 WHAT YOU DO AND WHAT SOMEONE ELSE DOES

Unlike in English, verbs or action words, for example **bekerja** *work* and **berasal** *originate from,* do not change depending on who is acting.

Saya bekerja dan Pak Jon bekerja. *I work and Mr Jon works.*

When verbs appear in different forms, it's because of the use of affixes, word parts that are combined with root words to make other words. In Conversation 1, Budi uses both **bekerja** and **kerja** to mean *work*. **ber-** is a prefix, or an affix attached to the start of a word. When the root word is a verb, such as **kerja** (*to work*), and there is no change in meaning, Indonesians will use either the root form or the proper form **bekerja** (*work*). However, the root word of **berasal** is the noun **asal** meaning *origin* and this is only a verb when it is **berasal** (*to originate/come from*).

> If the root word begins with **XerX** (where X is a consonant), such as **kerja** (*work*), the **ber-** prefix often loses its **r**, so that you end up with **bekerja** and not **berkerja.**

3 ASKING QUESTIONS

In Indonesian, there's no need to place question words such as, **mana** (*where*) and **apa** (*what*) at the start of the question.

Dari mana Anda berasal? (lit.) *From where do you come?*

Nama universitas Anda apa? (lit.) *Your university's name is what?*

However, **mana** (*where*) has to be used with the location word that matches the action. To ask where Jon came *from*, Budi used **dari mana**. To ask *in* what location Jon lives, Budi used **di mana**. Similarly, to ask where someone went *to*, you would use **ke mana**.

Practice

1 Put the following sentences into Indonesian.

a English is my mother tongue.
b I am working in an office.
c This is my colleague.
d Utomo is living in China.

2 Match the words to their root words.

a bekerja	**1** temu
b bertemu	**2** bahasa
c berasal	**3** kerja
d berbahasa	**4** asal

3 01.04 Read the questions below and prepare responses that are true for you. Then, listen and respond in real time.

a Anda berasal dari mana?
b Di mana Anda tinggal?
c Anda bekerja di mana?
d Apa nama bank Anda?

Pronunciation

01.05 Let's begin with one of the most common sounds in Indonesian. Say aloud the English word 'back' and pay attention to the release of air at the end. When saying Indonesian words that end in the letter 'k', pronounce that 'k' without the release of air or aspiration. **Listen to how the following words are pronounced and repeat.**

1 bapak
2 anak
3 masak
4 bebek

Speaking

01.06 Practice introducing yourself and others in Indonesian.

- **a** I'm ...
- **b** Let me introduce you. This is ...
- **c** My colleague is from ...

Conversation 2

01.07 *Linda is sightseeing in Jakarta and sees an Indonesian girl whom she then approaches.*

1 What is the name of the hotel?

Linda	Halo.
Girl	Halo.
Linda	Siapa nama kamu?
Girl	Nama aku Siti, Bu. Ibu siapa?
Linda	Aku Linda.
Girl	Ibu orang apa?
Linda	Aku orang Inggris. Siti, apa itu?
Girl	Itu hotel.
Linda	Apa nama hotel itu?
Girl	Hotel Indonesia.
Linda	Terima kasih.
Girl	Sama-sama.
Linda	Dah, Siti!
Girl	Dah, Bu Linda!

orang	*person*
Inggris	*England, English*

LANGUAGE TIP

When **Bu/Ibu** and **Pak/Bapak** are used on their own, they mean, respectively, *Madam* and *Sir.*

2 Find the expressions in the conversation that mean:

- **a** What is your name?
- **b** What is that?

c Thank you.
d You're welcome.

3 **Check, then cover up your answers and see if you can say them without looking at the conversation.**

4 **Read or listen again and answer the following questions.**
a What is the girl's name?
b Where is Linda from?
c Who is older or of higher status?
d Are they being formal or informal with each other?

5 **01.08 Now listen to the lines from the conversation and repeat. Then listen to Linda's lines and respond as Siti.**

Language discovery 2

Refer to the conversation and choose the correct word.

a *Apa / Siapa* nama kamu?
b Ibu orang *apa / siapa*?

1 WHO AND WHAT

You have now seen the question word **siapa** (*who*) used to ask for someone's name instead of the question word **apa** (*what*). This is a special case that applies only when asking for the names of humans, pets, or inanimate objects that have been given personal names by their owners. Note that when Linda asked for the name of the hotel, the word used was **apa** (*what*).

2 DESCRIBING YOURSELF

You can identify yourself and others as being a certain nationality, for example, British or American, by using the relevant place name with the word **orang** meaning *person*.

Kamu orang apa? Aku orang Inggris.

You are what kind of person? I am a British person.

Kamu orang apa? Aku orang Amerika.

What is your nationality? I am American.

LANGUAGE TIP

You can also use **orang** with a place name to talk about ethnicity so that **orang Bali** is a *Balinese person*.

Note that the question word **apa** (*what*) is placed after the noun **orang** (*person*), where the answer, in this case the place name, would be in your reply. In a question like this, the question word **apa** (*what*) needs to stay exactly where it is in relation to the word **orang** (*person*) or the question's meaning is lost. An alternative word order for this question is therefore,

Orang apa kamu? (lit.) *What kind of person are you?*

Practice

1 Give the Indonesian for the following questions.

a What is your name?

b What is the name of that university?

c Linda is English.

2 01.09 Practice asking and answering questions about your nationality.

Here are some countries you may come from:

Skotlandia	*Scotland*	**Wales**	*Wales*
Irlandia	*Ireland*	**Kanada**	*Canada*
Singapura	*Singapore*	**India**	*India*
Australia	*Australia*	**Selandia Baru**	*New Zealand*

Listening

pamit	*part* (v.)	**pergi**	*go*
sekarang	*now*	**belajar**	*study*

Listening

1 01.10 Listen to the following people as they greet or part from each other. Match each pair to the correct time of day.

a Kris and Maria	**1** 11:00 p.m.
b Wawan and Peter	**2** 06:00 a.m.
c Heryanto and Wati	**3** 01:30 p.m.
d Pingkan and Mimi	**4** 05:00 p.m.

You can also use greetings that are related to the time of day as farewells.

2 01.11 Listen to the recording and complete the social media profiles.

Name: ____________
Location: ____________
Hometown: ____________
Education: ____________

Name: ____________
Location: ____________
Hometown: ____________
Education: ____________

3 01.12 Read the questions below and prepare your own responses. Then, listen and respond in real time. Do this as many times as you need to for it to become second nature.

Di mana kamu belajar?

Aku belajar di Universitas Indonesia.

a Siapa nama kamu?
b Di mana kamu tinggal sekarang?
c Dari mana kamu berasal?

Reading and writing

1 Read the blog entry and answer the questions.

Blog

Search

Halo. Nama saya Alex Lasut. Saya orang Indonesia. Saya berasal dari Sulawesi dan tinggal di Cardiff sekarang. Saya bekerja di Universitas Wales. Saya juga belajar di universitas itu.

a Alex orang apa?
b Dari mana Alex berasal?
c Di mana Alex tinggal sekarang?
d Di mana Alex bekerja dan belajar?

2 Write a blog entry about yourself.

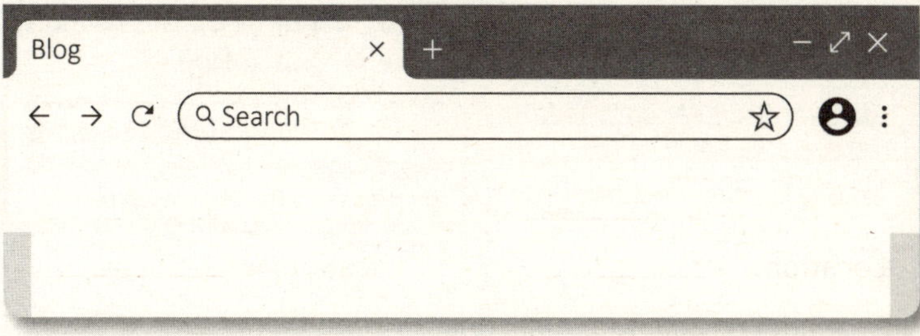

Go further

When using Indonesian, you will need to think about whether you should be formal or informal, respectfully distant or close. Informal pronouns such as **aku** (*I*) and **kamu** (*you*) are used when speaking to friends, people of equal or lower status, and children. Using formal pronouns such as **saya** (*I*) and **Anda** (*you*), on the other hand, demonstrates respect to the person you're speaking to, perhaps because they are older or of higher social status. Pronouns are also chosen to fit the occasion, for example when talking to people you've just met or in an office meeting. When in doubt, choose the formal pronouns.

Consider too that many Indonesians will be pleased to call you by your first name, but do not expect them to leave out the honorific **Bu** (*Ms/Mrs/Madam*) or **Pak** (*Mr/Sir*) unless they are older, of higher status, or a close friend. If you are an Emma or a Tom, for example, do get used to being **Bu Emma** or **Pak Tom**.

Indonesians might also describe themselves according to their regional or ethnic identity, whether due to their mother tongue, where their ancestors are from, or where they have spent most of their lives. Here are some of the larger ethnic classifications:

1 Match the Indonesian to the English.

a orang Jawa	**1** Madurese
b orang Sunda	**2** Batak
c orang Melayu	**3** Sundanese
d orang Madura	**4** Malay
e orang Batak	**5** Javanese

2 01.13 **Read the questions below and prepare appropriate responses. Then, listen and respond in real time. Do this as many times as you need to for it to become second nature.**

a Pramoedya Ananta Toer orang apa?

b Siapa belajar bahasa Indonesia?

Before the 1970s, the letter **u** was mainly spelled as **oe** in Indonesian. This spelling can still be found in Indonesian names.

Test yourself

1 Match the greeting to the times.

a Selamat siang. — **1** *09:00 a.m.*

b Selamat sore. — **2** *11:00 a.m.*

c Selamat pagi. — **3** *11:00 p.m.*

d Selamat malam. — **4** *05:00 p.m.*

2 Give the English for the following sentences.

a Kamu kerja di mana?

b Saya bekerja di universitas.

c Bambang bekerja di Jepang.

3 Correct the underlined words.

a Kamu belajar <u>dari</u> mana?

b Ibu Hitomi berasal <u>ke</u> mana?

c Anda pergi <u>di</u> mana?

4 Complete the sentences.

a _______ nama kamu?

b _______ nama hotel Anda?

c _______ orang itu?

d Pak Dinesh orang _______?

5 Translate the following sentences into Indonesian.

a I am a Scot.

b My colleague is a New Zealander.

c What is your nationality?

d Where is Ms Rosa from?

SELF CHECK

I CAN . . .
. . . use greetings that suit the time of day.
. . . introduce myself and others.
. . . say where I am from, where I live, and where I work or study.
. . . use the appropriate pronouns when talking to others.
. . . thank others and respond to thanks.

2

In this unit, you will learn how to:

» use the appropriate pronouns when talking about others.

» ask and answer yes/no questions.

» talk about events happening earlier or later in the day.

» ask for and give phone numbers.

Siapa dia?

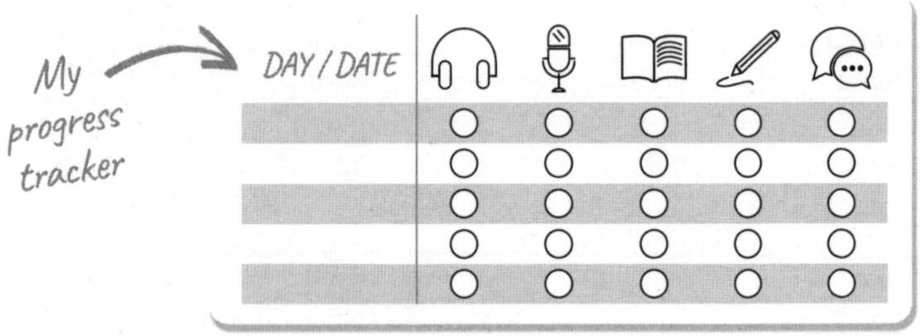

Community

Many Indonesians enjoy socializing through a shared interest in an activity, whether it is cultural, recreational, or a sport. There are a variety of clubs at university for a student to join and where they can **bermain catur** (*play chess*), **menari** (*dance*), or **mendaki gunung** (*do mountain climbing*). It is in these clubs, and at their weekend trips and get-togethers, that a **kenalan** (*acquaintance*) can turn into a lifelong **teman** (*friend*). Outside the formal education system but equally important, there are local organizations where **orang-orang muda** (*young people*) can learn from their elders about **bermain musik tradisional** (*playing traditional music*) or **berlatih pencak silat** (*training in Indonesian martial arts*). A **kampung** (*village*), whether rural or urban, will have social events and cultural activities through which an Indonesian can mingle and get to know **tetangga dia** (*his/her neighbor*). Communities also hold **sepak bola** (*football*) and **bulu tangkis** (*badminton*) games, usually to celebrate Independence Day on the 17th of August, and all residents can participate as players or spectators. People who enjoy **berselam skuba** (*scuba diving*) and **berselancar** (*surfing*) may have to go to the coast or travel to the archipelago's smaller islands, but there enthusiasts can also gather and develop a sense of community that is very important in Indonesian life.

How would you say *playing football* in Indonesian?

Vocabulary builder

02.01 Look at the words and phrases and complete the English translations of contrasting adjectives. Then listen to the recording and imitate the pronunciation of the speakers.

ADJECTIVES

ramah	*friendly*	**sombong**	*snobbish*
lama	*old, of long duration*	**baru**	*new*
tua	______	**muda**	*young*
tinggi	*tall*	**pendek**	______

NEUTRAL PRONOUNS

dia	*he/she, him/her, his/her*
kami	*we/us/our (exclusive)*
kita	*we/us/our (inclusive)*

NUMBERS

0	nol *or* kosong	5	lima
1	satu	6	enam
2	dua	7	tujuh
3	tiga	8	delapan
4	empat	9	sembilan

NEW EXPRESSIONS

Apakah	(interrogative in yes/no questions)
ya	*yes*
juga	*too, also*
bukan	*no, not*
pulau	*island*
tidak	*no, not*
senang	*enjoy*
Ayo!	*Come! / Come on!*
kepada	*to (someone)*

harus	*must*
tadi	*earlier*
nanti	*later*
berapa	*how many*
nomor telpon	*phone number*

Conversation 1

02.02 *Wati has brought Linda, who is talking to others, to a street party. Affandi is Wati's neighbor.*

1 What did Linda and Wati do on the island of Bangka?

Affandi	Selamat malam, Wati.
Wati	Selamat malam. Apakah Anda Affandi?
Affandi	Ya. Saya Affandi.
Wati	Kita bertetangga?
Affandi	Ya. Saya tetangga baru Anda. Wati, saya tidak kenal orang itu. Apakah dia tetangga kita juga?
Wati	Bukan. Dia bukan tetangga kita.
Affandi	Siapa dia?
Wati	Dia Linda, teman lama saya. Kami berkenalan di Bangka. Kami berselam skuba di pulau itu.
Affandi	Linda ramah?
Wati	Ya, Linda ramah. Dia tidak sombong.
Affandi	Dia senang apa?
Wati	Dia senang mendaki gunung dan berselam skuba. Dan Affandi?
Affandi	Saya senang mendaki gunung juga.
Wati	Ayo! Saya kenalkan Affandi kepada Linda.

bertetangga	*to be/become neighbors*
kenal	*recognize, know*
senang, gemar	*enjoy, be pleased*

2 Find the expressions in the conversation that mean:

- **a** I am your new neighbor.
- **b** Who is she?
- **c** What does she enjoy?
- **d** Come on!

3 Check, then cover up your answers and see if you can say them without looking at the conversation.

4 Read the conversation or listen again and answer the questions.

- **a** Around what time of day is it?
- **b** Is Linda their neighbor too?
- **c** Who enjoys mountain climbing?
- **d** What is Wati going to do?

5 02.03 **Now listen to the lines from the conversation and repeat. Be sure to pay attention to the pronunciation.**

Language discovery 1

Look at the sentences from the conversation. Put the words in English into Indonesian.

- **a** Dia Linda, (*my old friend*).
- **b** (*We*) bertetangga. (*We*) berselam skuba di pulau itu.
- **c** Dia (*not*) tetangga kita. Dia (*not*) sombong.

1 WORD ORDER

In Indonesian, an adjective will come after the word it describes so that a *new friend* is a **teman baru.** When arranging the word order in a longer noun phrase such as *my old friend*, the order in Indonesian will be the reverse of the order in English so that you would say **teman lama saya**.

2 *WE*

Unlike other pronouns, **kita** or **kami** is used to mean *we, us, our* depending on whom you include or exclude from the grouping. You can use **kita** (*we, us*) when the person you're speaking to is included and **kami** when they are not. Linda used **kita** when she asked Affandi, **Kita bertetangga?** (*Are we neighbors?*) because he was included in the *we*. Linda used **kami** to mean Wati and herself, while telling Affandi, **Kami berkenalan di Bangka** (*We became acquainted in Bangka*) because he was not included in the *we*.

3 ASKING AND ANSWERING YES/NO QUESTIONS

You can turn statements into yes/no questions using **apakah** (*whether, if*) as the question word **Apakah**. If you are familiar with how a question sounds, you can leave out **Apakah**.

Kamu Affandi.	*You are Affandi.*
Apakah kamu Affandi? Kamu Affandi?	*Are you Affandi?*

To express *yes* in Indonesian, you can use the word **ya**.

Ya, saya Affandi.	*Yes, I am Affandi.*

There are two different Indonesian words for *no/not*. The word **tidak** is used to negate verbs and adjectives. The word **bukan** is used to negate nouns, including names and pronouns. They are both placed before what you are negating in the sentence.

Tidak. Aku tidak berselancar.	*No. I do not surf.*
Tidak. Dia tidak tinggi.	*No. He is not tall.*
Bukan. Dia bukan Affandi.	*No. He is not Affandi.*

Practice

1 Put the following sentences into English.

a kenalan baru saya
b teman pendek kami
c tetangga lama kita

2 Choose the correct word.

a *Kita / Kami* bermain catur. (*said to Shinta, including Shinta*)
b *Kita / Kami* menari. (*said to Shinta, not including Shinta*)

3 02.04 Turn the statements below into yes/no questions using *apakah* **and prepare your own responses. Then, listen and respond in real time.**

a Anda berlatih pencak silat di Indonesia.
b Anda orang Indonesia.
c Anda tinggi.

Pronunciation

02.05 The consonant *ng* is found in English at the end and middle of words, such as in 'singing' and 'mingle', but in Indonesian it is also found at the start of words. Listen to how the following words are pronounced and repeat.

1 singa

2 tetangga

3 mangga

4 ngantuk

5 nganga

If you're having trouble with words that begin with **ng**, try, for example, to say <u>Singapura</u> (*Singapore*) and then practice omitting the **si** at the beginning.

Speaking

02.06 Practice telling others about one of your friends and tell them about what you and your friend enjoy doing together. Use what you know instead of looking up new words. Here are some other activities to help you.

berenang	*swimming*
membaca	*reading*
minum-minum	*drinking (alcoholic beverages)*
makan-makan	*eating (for pleasure)*

Dia ... Dia orang ... Kami senang ...

Conversation 2

02.07 *Budi and Jon meet again but Jon is in a rush. Budi would like Jon's phone number.*

1 What is Jon's phone number?

Budi	Anda harus berbuat apa sekarang?
Jon	Saya harus bekerja sekarang. Saya berselancar tadi pagi. Nanti malam kita bertemu lagi?
Budi	Saya berlatih pencak silat nanti malam. Anda senang pencak silat?
Jon	Ya. Saya senang pencak silat.
Budi	Berapa nomor telpon Anda?
Jon	Nomor telpon saya kosong – delapan – satu – satu – tujuh – empat – enam – dua – lima – tiga – dua – sembilan.
Budi	Ini nomor ponsel Pak Jon?
Jon	Ya. Itu nomor ponsel saya.
Budi	Saya menelpon Pak Jon nanti sore.
Jon	Sampai nanti sore.

berbuat	*do (something)*
ponsel	*cell phone*
menelpon	*call* (v.), *ring* (v.)

Indonesians are fond of acronyms, so much so that there are whole dictionaries devoted to them. One popular acronym for the *cell phone*, **ponsel**, is taken from the last syllable of **telpon** and the first syllable of **seluler**. Equally widespread is **HP**, short for *hand phone*.

2 Match the Indonesian to the English.

a tadi pagi	**1** *later tonight*
b sekarang	**2** *later this afternoon*
c nanti sore	**3** *earlier this morning*
d nanti malam	**4** *now*

3 Read or listen again and answer the following questions.

a When did Jon go surfing?

b When is Budi practicing martial arts?

c When will Budi call Jon?

d What time of day do you think it is?

4 02.08 Now listen to the lines from the conversation and repeat. Then listen to Budi's lines and respond as Jon.

Language discovery 2

Look at the sentences from the conversation. Find the words in Indonesian for the words in English.

a Saya berselancar (*earlier this morning*).

b (*What*) nomor telepon Anda? Saya menelpon (*you*) nanti sore.

1 LATER AND EARLIER

You can use the words **nanti** (*later*) and **tadi** (*earlier*) on their own, but Indonesians also combine them with the times of day to talk about different time periods in that day.

tadi pagi	*earlier in the morning* (dawn to 10 a.m.)
tadi siang	*earlier during the day* (10 a.m. to 3 p.m.)
tadi sore	*earlier in the afternoon* (3 p.m. to 6 p.m.)
nanti siang	*later during the day* (10 a.m. to 3 p.m.)
nanti sore	*later in the afternoon* (3 p.m. to 6 p.m.)
nanti malam	*later in the evening, later tonight* (after sunset)

Note that you cannot say **nanti pagi** (*later in the morning*) but you can say **tadi malam** to mean *last night*.

2 ASKING FOR A PHONE NUMBER

The question word **berapa** (*how many*) is used whenever the answer is a number, even when there is no counting involved. When asking for a phone number, you would use **berapa** instead of **apa** (*what*).

3 USING SOMEONE'S NAME TO MEAN *YOU*

Often, **Anda** and **kamu** (*you*) can be replaced with the name of the person being spoken to. For example, Budi switched from using **Anda** to **Pak Jon** to mean *you* towards the end of Conversation 2. Budi asked **Ini nomor ponsel Pak Jon?** *This is Mr Jon's cell phone number?* to actually mean *This is your cell phone number?* It is a way of speaking that is useful when social status is unclear or when formal pronouns prohibit a sense of closeness and friendliness.

Practice

1 **Put the following sentences into Indonesian.**

- **a** I was playing traditional music earlier this morning and last night.
- **b** Earlier during the day, she and Budi played chess.

2 **02.09 First, practice asking and answering questions about your phone number. Then, replace** *Anda* **or** *kamu* **in the question with your name and practice again.**

Listening

rumah	*house, home*	**teras**	*porch*
halaman	*yard, garden*	**sekolah**	*school*

1 **02.10 Listen to the dialogue and answer the following questions.**

- **a** Where did they play football?
- **b** Where are they playing chess?
- **c** When will they go out to eat?

2 **02.11 Listen to the recording and write down Ratna's phone numbers.**

> *Ratna HP:* ______________________________
> *Kantor:* ______________________________
> *Rumah:* ______________________________

3 **02.12 Read the questions below and prepare your own responses. Then, listen and respond in real time. Do this as many times as you need to for it to become second nature.**

- **a** Apakah teman kamu muda?
- **b** Kamu harus berbuat apa sekarang?
- **c** Berapa nomor telepon kamu?

Reading and writing

1 Linda is currently living in Indonesia. She has written a blog post about her time in Indonesia so far. To practice her language skills, she has chosen to write it in Indonesian. Read the post and check the glossary if there are words you don't know.

Blog Add post

Halo dari Indonesia!

Wati adalah teman lama saya. Saya berkenalan dengan Wati di Pulau Bangka di mana kami berselam skuba. Wati orang Sunda. Dia dari Bandung. Dia tinggi, gemuk, dan ramah. Kami senang menari dan bermain musik tradisional. Tadi malam saya pergi ke rumah dia di kampung Kauman. Kami menari dan makan-makan di rumah tetangga dia. Saya berkenalan dengan Affandi. Dia teman baru saya. Nanti sore kami bermain bulu tangkis.

Sampai nanti!

2 Imagine you are writing a blog post about your time in Indonesia. Describe your Indonesian friends and how you met them.

Blog Add post

Go further

Like the neutral pronoun **dia**, the very formal **beliau** is used to talk about both male (*he/him/his*) and female (*she/her*) others. However, it's most often used in the news or when referring to someone of much higher status, such as a venerable elder. In everyday formal situations, using the person's name instead of pronouns when referring to them is more common.

Beliau kepala negara di negara ini.

He/She is the head of state in this country.

In this unit, you've seen verbs that begin with the prefix **meX-**, such as **menelpon** (*ring*) and **mendaki** (*climb*). The **X** in **meX-** stands for a consonant that changes depending on the root word. (If you'd like to read ahead about how the consonants change, you can go to Unit 8.) The prefix **meX-** is generally used when the verb describes an action that involves more than just the actor. For example, you ring *someone* and you climb *something*.

You now know that the word **senang** can mean *to enjoy* and *to be pleased*. If an activity *pleases* you because it is fun or pleasurable, you can say it is **menyenangkan** (*pleasing*).

1 Use the words in the box to recreate the sentences below.

senang, bermain, ke, senang, saya, Indonesia, saya, menyenangkan, pergi, gamelan

a I am pleased.
b Playing gamelan is fun.
c I enjoy going to Indonesia.

There are many different instruments in Indonesian traditional music. One of the most impressive is the **gamelan**, which is actually an ensemble of percussions. Another is the Sundanese **angklung**, a set of bamboo tubes arranged on a frame and shaken to produce repeating notes.

2 02.13 Read the questions below and prepare your own responses. Then, listen and respond. Do this as many times as you need to for it to become second nature.

a Apakah musik tradisional negara Anda menyenangkan?
b Apakah bertemu orang Indonesia menyenangkan?

Test yourself

1 Put the following sentences into Indonesian.

a He is my new neighbor.

b This is her school's phone number.

c That is your schoolyard.

2 Imagine you are speaking to Jon. Use the correct form of *we* to replace the words in English.

a (*You and I*) berlatih pencak silat nanti malam.

b (*Wati and I*) berasal dari Indonesia.

c (*You and I*) berteman.

3 Put the words in English into Indonesian.

a (*No.*) Saya (*not*) bermain catur.

b Teman kami (*not*) tua.

c (*No*). Dia (*not*) tetangga saya.

4 Match the Indonesian to the English.

a tadi sore	**1** *later this evening*
b nanti sore	**2** *earlier this afternoon*
c tadi malam	**3** *later this afternoon*
d nanti malam	**4** *last night*

5 Complete the English translations.

a nomor telepon	*phone* __________
b ponsel	__________
c Berapa nomor HP Anda?	__________

6 Imagine you are asking Linda the following questions. Where possible, replace the pronouns with her name.

a Ke mana aku dan kamu pergi sekarang?

b Di mana dia bertemu kamu nanti?

c Anda dan beliau berselam skuba di mana?

SELF CHECK

	I CAN . . .
○	. . . use the appropriate pronouns when talking about others.
○	. . . ask and answer yes/no questions.
○	. . . talk about events happening earlier or later in the day.
○	. . . ask for and give phone numbers.

3

In this unit, you will learn how to:

» ask and answer questions about how you and others are.
» talk about your family.
» indicate whether you have or have not done something.
» make a phone call, and leave and take a message.
» indicate if you are (not) following the conversation.

Apa kabar keluarga Anda?

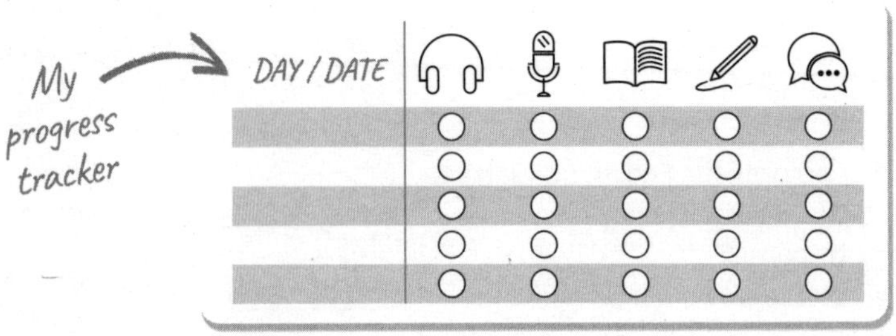

Family

Contemporary Indonesian society, with the **keluarga** (*family*) at its heart, remains shaped by traditional values and gender roles. It is generally assumed that most people will marry one day and have **anak-anak** (*children*). When Indonesians ask whether someone is **belum menikah** (*not yet married*) or **sudah menikah** (*already married*) not long after meeting them for the first time, they would not think of themselves as nosy or forward. This is perhaps easier for someone to **mengerti** (*understand*) when they know that questions about their marital status are meant to reflect an interest in their life's fulfilment. It is thought that to become a **bapak** or **ayah** (*father*) and **ibu** (*mother*) is to realize one's potential as a **laki-laki** (*man, male*) and a **perempuan** (*woman, female*). Public health programs advocate having only **dua anak** (*two children*), but having more children is common because a large family is thought to be a blessing. This includes having several generations living together, with offspring continuing to share a household with their **orang tua** (*parents*) even after marriage or staying nearby so that both the **kakek** (*grandfather*) and **nenek** (*grandmother*) have a role in the upbringing of children.

If **anak** is the word for child and **anak-anak** is the word for children, what do you think the word for families might be in Indonesian?

Vocabulary builder

03.01 Look at the words and phrases and complete the English translations. Then listen to the recording and imitate the pronunciation of the speakers.

FAMILY MEMBERS	
suami	*husband*
istri	*wife*
adik	*younger sibling*
adik-adik	________
kakak	*older sibling*
kakak-kakak	________
cucu	*grandchild*
cucu-cucu	________

The all-encompassing word **saudara** (*relative/sibling*) also signals close ties between people who are only distantly related or who are not related by blood.

TEMPORAL MARKERS	
sudah	*already*
belum	*not yet*
masih	*still*

TIME	
hari ini	*today* (lit. *this day*)
kemarin	*yesterday*
besok	*tomorrow*

PLURAL PRONOUN	
mereka	*they, them, their*

NEW EXPRESSIONS	
Apa kabar?	*How are you?* (lit. *What news?*)
Kabar baik.	*I'm well.* (lit. *Good news.*)

Kasihan!	*What a pity!, Poor thing!*
punya	*have, possess, own*
Oh begitu.	*Oh I see.* (lit. *Oh it's like that.*)
bisa	*can, able to*
bicara	*speak, converse*
dengan	*with*
titip pesan	*leave/entrust a message*
Tolong ulang	*Please repeat*
sekali lagi	*one more time* (lit. *once more*)
Baiklah.	*All right., Okay.*

Conversation 1

03.02 *Budi and Jon meet again and find out more about each other.*

1 Who is not yet married?

Jon	Selamat siang, Pak Budi.
Budi	Selamat siang, Pak Jon.
Jon	Apa kabar?
Budi	Kabar baik, Pak Jon. Dan Anda?
Jon	Saya baik juga. Apa kabar keluarga Anda?
Budi	Anak saya baik. Istri saya tidak baik kemarin.
Jon	Kasihan! Beliau masih sakit hari ini?
Budi	Tidak. Dia sudah sembuh. Dia baik pagi ini.
Jon	Bagus!
Budi	Pak Jon sudah menikah?
Jon	Belum. Saya belum menikah.
Budi	Oh begitu. Orang tua Pak Jon di Inggris sudah punya cucu?
Jon	Sudah. Mereka sudah punya cucu-cucu. Kakak laki-laki saya sudah punya tiga anak perempuan.
Budi	Bagus! Di mana mereka tinggal?
Jon	Keluarga kakak saya tinggal di Irlandia.

baik	*good, well*
bagus	*good, well done*
sakit	*ill, sick*
sembuh	*recover, get well again*

2 Find the expressions in the conversation that mean:

a Poor thing!

b How are you?

c Good!

d How is your family?

3 Check, then cover up your answers and see if you can say them without looking at the conversation.

4 Read the conversation or listen again and answer the questions.

a Around what time of day is it?

b Who was unwell?

c How many grandchildren do Jon's parents have?

d Who lives in Ireland?

5 03.03 Now listen to the lines from the conversation and repeat. Be sure to pay attention to the pronunciation.

Language discovery 1

1 Look at the sentences from the conversation. Put the words in English into Indonesian.

a Kabar (*good*). **b** Saya (*well*) juga. **c** (*Good*)!

2 Refer to the conversation. Put the following sentences into Indonesian.

a I am not yet married.

b They already have grandchildren.

1 ASKING AND RESPONDING TO HOW OTHERS ARE

When you ask someone how they are, you're asking for their **kabar** (*news*). If someone is *well* or their news is *good,* they will use the word **baik**, which is generally used to talk about wellness, niceness, and things humans can't control, such as one's news. To give a positive response to someone's news, you can use the word **bagus** (*good*), which is used when praising human achievements, products, or favourable developments, such as being well or recovering from an illness. When you want to express sympathy about others, you can say **Kasihan!** (*Poor thing!*) When you want to give a neutral reply, you can say **Oh begitu** (*Oh it's like that*) to mean *Oh I see.*

2 WHAT HAS OR HAS NOT HAPPENED

Whether something has happened, is still happening, or has not yet happened, the Indonesian verb stays the same. In order to be able to express these different states, you should use temporal markers before the verb, such as **sudah** (*already*), **masih** (*still*), and **belum** (*not yet*).

As in English, the words **sudah** (*already*) and **belum** (*not yet*) negate each other. When you want to use **tidak** (*not*) with a marker, you place it before the marker.

Saya belum bekerja.	*I have not worked yet.*
Saya masih bekerja.	*I am still working.*
Saya sudah bekerja.	*I already worked.*
Saya tidak masih bekerja.	*I am not still working.*

At social gatherings, Indonesians may greet you by asking **Sudah makan?** meaning *Have you eaten?*

Practice

1 Put the following sentences into English.

a Apa kabar?

b Saya baik.

c Apa kabar mereka?

2 03.04 Read the questions below and prepare your own responses. Then, listen and respond in real time.

a Anda sudah menikah?

b Anda belum punya cucu?

Pronunciation

03.05 When *ai* and *au* are found in syllables that end in a vowel, they form combinations so that *ai* sounds like the vowel in 'pie' and *au* sounds like the vowel in 'how'. When *ai* and *au* are found in syllables that end in a consonant, however, they don't form a combination and are pronounced separately instead. Listen to how the following words are pronounced and repeat.

1 sampai	**2** bagaimana	**3** baik
4 saudara	**5** beliau	**6** laut

Speaking

1 03.06 Look at the family tree and describe each relationship in a sentence.

Edwin dan Mutia orang tua Hendri.

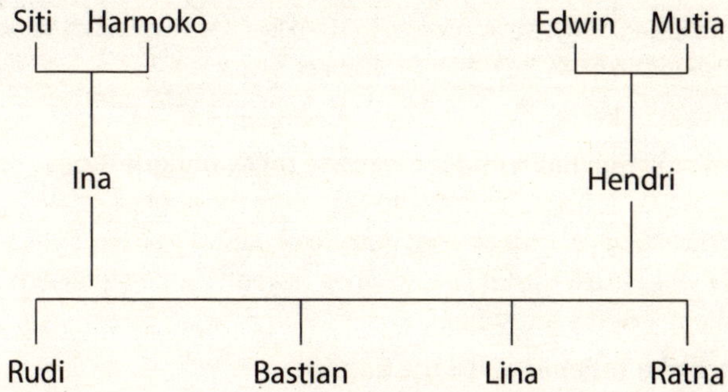

2 Dan keluarga Anda? *And what about your family?* **Describe the same relationships between people in your family.**

Conversation 2

03.07 *Budi is calling Jon, but Saul answers instead.*

1 Who is Saul?

Budi	Halo. Bisa bicara dengan Pak Jon?
Saul	Halo. Tidak bisa. Jon masih bekerja. Dengan siapa saya berbicara?
Budi	Ini Budi.
Saul	Oh, Pak Budi! Anda teman kakak saya.
Budi	Oh saya tidak tahu Pak Jon punya adik di Indonesia.
Saul	Ya. Jon punya dua adik. Saya tinggal di Indonesia juga dan Thomas tinggal di Inggris.
Budi	Oh begitu. Saya bisa menitip pesan?
Saul	Saya tidak mengerti. Tolong ulang sekali lagi.
Budi	Bisa titip pesan? *Can I leave a message?*
Saul	Saya mengerti sekarang. Bisa. Apa pesan Anda?
Budi	Tolong bilang, 'Budi menelpon Pak Jon besok.'
Saul	Baiklah. Nanti saya sampaikan.
Budi	Terima kasih.
Saul	Sama-sama.

tahu	*know, be aware (of)*
Halo	(phone greeting)
bilang	*say*
sampaikan	*pass (something) on*

The word **bilang** is used to mean *say* only in colloquial speech or speech-like writing. You would otherwise use **berkata** to mean *say*.

2 Read or listen again and answer the following questions.

a Why was Jon not the one who answered the phone?
b How many younger siblings does Jon have?
c What did Saul ask Budi to do when he didn't understand him?
d What is Budi's message?

3 Match the Indonesian to the English.

a Bisa bicara dengan Pak Jon?	**1** *All right.*
b Saya tidak mengerti.	**2** *Can I leave a message?*
c Bisa titip pesan?	**3** *I don't understand.*
d Baiklah.	**4** *Can I speak to Mr Jon?*

4 03.08 Now listen to the lines from the conversation and repeat. Then listen to Budi's lines and respond as Saul.

Language discovery 2

Refer to the conversation and put the following sentences into Indonesian.

a I will call him tomorrow.
b two younger siblings
c Please say, 'I understand now'.

1 THE IMPORTANCE OF TIME WORDS

As you may have noticed, Indonesian verbs do not change in response to time. There are no tenses to worry about, but you do then have to rely on words like **kemarin** (*yesterday*), **hari ini** (*today*), and **besok** (*tomorrow*) to make your meaning clear.

2 PLURALS AND NUMBERS

To create the plural form, you simply repeat the noun, adding a hyphen between them in written Indonesian. For example, **cucu** is *grandchild* and **cucu-cucu** is *grandchildren*. This is known as reduplication or doubling and is done only when no quantity is defined. For example, **istri-istri** means *wives* but **tiga istri** means *three wives* and **satu istri** means *one wife*.

3 MAKING A PHONE CALL AND LEAVING A MESSAGE

Indonesians answer the phone using **halo** (*hello*), but there is no specific parting phrase to use. If you want to *leave a message*, you simply ask if you can **titip pesan** (*leave/entrust a message*) and start your message with **Tolong bilang ...** (*Please say ...*) If you're taking a message, you can assure others by saying **nanti saya sampaikan** to mean *I'll pass it on (later)*.

Practice

1 Put the following sentences into Indonesian.

- **a** I called my older brother yesterday.
- **b** I will call my younger sister today.
- **c** I will pass on your message tomorrow.

2 Choose the correct word.

- **a** Dua *anak / anak-anak* kami tinggal di Bandung.
- **b** Berapa *kantor / kantor-kantor* (*offices*) mereka?

3 03.09 Practice leaving and taking a message over the phone.

Listening

banyak	*much, many*
sedikit	*a few, a little*

1 03.10 Listen to the dialogue and answer the following questions.

- **a** Is Wati well?
- **b** Is Wati married?
- **c** In whose house does her family live?

Anak aku dua (*My children are two in number*) is another way of saying *I have two children.*

2 03.11 **Listen to the recording and write down the message and who it is from in English.**

Message:	*From:*

3 03.12 **Read the questions below and prepare your own responses. Then, listen and respond in real time. Do this as many times as you need to for it to become second nature.**

a Apa kabar?

b Apa kabar keluarga Anda?

c Apakah Anda mengerti sedikit bahasa Indonesia?

Reading and writing

1 **Harjeet Singh has sent an email to his Indonesian penfriend Anisa Rusli about his family. Read the email and check the glossary if there are words you don't know.**

New message

Halo Anisa!

Apa kabar? Apa kabar keluarga kamu?

Kabar saya dan keluarga saya baik. Saya dan orang tua saya tinggal di Mumbles, Wales. Ayah saya dokter. Ibu saya manajer hotel. Nenek saya, Tripta, tinggal di rumah kami juga. Saya punya dua kakak. Kakak perempuan saya tinggal di Cardiff dan dia punya satu anak. Kakak laki-laki saya belum menikah. Dia tinggal di Cardiff juga. Oh ya, nenek saya berasal dari India. Saya senang bicara dengan sepupu-sepupu saya di India.

Salam,
Harjeet

2 **Imagine you are writing a letter to your Indonesian penfriend. Describe your family using what you know.**

Go further

MORE FAMILY MEMBERS

anak tiri	*stepchild*
saudara tiri	*stepsibling, half-sibling*
kakak tiri	*older stepsibling/half-sibling*
adik tiri	*younger stepsibling/half-sibling*
anak angkat	*adopted child*
bibi, tante	*aunt*
paman, om	*uncle*
sepupu	*cousin*
keponakan	*niece, nephew*
pasangan	*partner*
pacar	*girlfriend, boyfriend*

You know that in Indonesian the words **Pak** (*Sir*) and Bu (*Madam*) are short for **Bapak** and **Ibu**, respectively. When you use either of them, you are in effect addressing someone as **bapak** (*father*) and **ibu** (*mother*). In Indonesia, people don't have to be actual relatives to address each other using words that in English are reserved only for family. A young customer might address an older shopkeeper as **Kak**, short for **Kakak** (*older sibling*), or **Bi**, short for **Bibi** (*aunt*), for example.

The words **tante** (*aunt*) and **om** (*uncle*) are mostly used in cities and higher socioeconomic classes. They are also often used to address people who are not from Indonesia. Instead of using **Pak** (*Sir*) and **Bu** (*Madam*), Indonesians might address non-Indonesians who are older than them as **Om** (*Uncle*) to mean *Sir* and **Tante** (*Aunt*) to mean *Madam*.

If you want to say that there is *much* or there are *many* of something without using numbers, use the word **banyak**.

Terima kasih banyak.

Thank you (very much).

Dia punya banyak sepupu.

She has many cousins.

The word **sedikit** is used to mean *a few* or *a little*.

Saya bisa bicara sedikit bahasa Arab.

I can speak a little Arabic.

1 03.13 Read the questions below and prepare your own responses. Then, listen and respond in real time. Do this as many times as you need to for it to become second nature.

- **a** Anda punya banyak saudara?
- **b** Anda bisa bicara bahasa Indonesia?

Test yourself

1 Use the words in the box to recreate the dialogue below.

baik, dan, kabar, bagus, Anda, baik, apa, juga, kabar, saya

- **a** How are you?
- **b** I'm well. And you?
- **c** I'm well too.
- **d** Good!

2 Match the Indonesian to the English.

a sudah menikah	1 *not yet married*
b belum menikah	2 *still married*
c masih menikah	3 *already married*

3 Put the words in English into Indonesian.

- **a** Saya (*not yet*) pergi ke bank (*today*).
- **b** Ibu aku (*already*) menelpon nenek kamu (*yesterday*).
- **c** Hari ini saya tidak (*still*) bekerja.
- **d** (*Tomorrow*) mereka masih belajar.

4 Put the following words into Indonesian.

- **a** houses
- **b** five families
- **c** eight children

5 Complete the English translations.

a	Bisa sampaikan pesan saya?	Can you ________ my ________?
b	Tolong bilang saya pergi.	Please ________ I am going.
c	Saya tidak mengerti.	I do not ________ .
d	Tolong ulang sekali lagi.	______________________ .

SELF CHECK

	I CAN . . .
○	. . . ask and answer questions about how I am and how others are.
○	. . . talk about my family.
○	. . . indicate whether I have or have not done something.
○	. . . make a phone call, and leave and take a message.
○	. . . indicate if I am (not) following the conversation.

R1

Review 1

1 Give the greetings or partings that suit the time of day.

a 8:00am

b 1:00pm

c 5:00pm

d 10:00pm

2 Provide the English translations.

a I/me/my _______ (formal), _______ (informal)

b you/your _______ (formal), _______ (informal)

c he/she/him/his/her _______ (neutral)

d we/us/our _______ (inclusive), _______ (exclusive)

e they, them, their _______ (neutral)

3 Put the following useful expressions into Indonesian.

a Thank you.

b You're welcome.

c Excuse me.

d Until we meet again.

e Can I speak to Ms Taraji?

4 Choose the correct words to check your knowledge of questions and question words.

a Nama kamu *siapa / apa*?

b *Mana / Dari mana* kamu berasal?

c *Di mana / Dari mana* kamu tinggal?

d *Siapa / Apa* nama sekolah kamu?

e Kamu pergi *di mana / ke mana* tadi malam?

5 Put the words in English into Indonesian.

a (*This*) Pak Budi. Dia (*works*) di Universitas Palembang.

b (*That*) Pak Jon. Pak Jon (*tall*). Dia (*friend*) baru Pak Budi. Dia (*English person*). Dia tahu (*Indonesian language*).

c Linda dan Wati (*enjoy*) berselam skuba.

d Affandi (*Linda's new neighbor*). Dia (*Indonesian person*). Dia tidak (*recognize/know*) Wati.

e Harjeet (*lives*) di Wales. (*His grandfather*) berasal (*from*) India.

6 Give negative answers to the following questions.

- **a** Apakah dia orang Selandia Baru?
- **b** Mereka berlatih pencak silat tadi siang?
- **c** Apakah suami Anda pendek?
- **d** Kamu menelpon orang tua kamu?

7 Match the Indonesian expressions to the English.

a Saya tidak mengerti.	**1** *Please repeat once more.*
b Tolong ulang sekali lagi.	**2** *I will pass it on.*
c Bisa titip pesan?	**3** *What is your message?*
d Apa pesan Anda?	**4** *Can I leave a message?*
e Nanti saya sampaikan.	**5** *I don't understand.*

8 Check your understanding of how to talk to others about numbers and plurals by putting the following in English.

- **a** Berapa nomor telepon Anisa?
- **b** Nomor telepon aku tujuh-dua-lima-enam-nol-empat-satu-sembilan.
- **c** Aku punya delapan anak. Anak-anak aku tinggal di Solo.
- **d** Berapa saudara Anda?
- **e** Saudara saya tiga.

9 Use the words in the box to recreate the phrases below.

belajar, tadi, sudah, nanti, anak, belum, pagi, masih, bekerja, punya

- **a** already studied earlier this morning
- **b** still working later
- **c** do not have a child yet

10 Match the statements or questions to the replies.

a Apa kabar?	1 Tolong bilang ...
b Saya baik.	2 Kasihan!
c Saya tidak baik.	3 Kabar baik.
d Apa pesan kamu?	4 Bagus!

11 **Ying sent a few text messages today. Read the messages and choose the correct answers.**

Aku belum makan.

a Ying *already ate / has not eaten yet.*

Tante kami bermain sepak bola tadi malam.

b Ying's *aunt / uncle* played football *last night / this morning.*

Besok aku bekerja di rumah.

c Tomorrow Ying is working at *home / the office.*

12 **Suteja keeps a blog about his life in Indonesia. Read this entry about his family and answer the following questions.**

Blog Add post

Orang tua saya sekarang tinggal dengan adik laki-laki saya, Koes, di Jakarta. Nenek dan kakek saya tinggal dengan sepupu saya di Bandung. Saya tinggal di Bandung juga. Saya dan sepupu saya belajar di universitas di Bandung. Kemarin saya pergi ke rumah nenek dan kakek. Saya dan kakek bermain musik tradisional Sunda di teras rumah mereka.

a Who lives with Suteja's parents?
b Who lives in Bandung?
c When did Suteja go to his grandparents' house?
d What did he do there?

4

In this unit, you will learn how to:

» talk about daily activities.
» use the days of the week to talk about an event or a habit.
» talk about what you and others do for a living.
» ask for and give ages.
» count people, animals, and large objects.

Anda berbuat apa setiap hari?

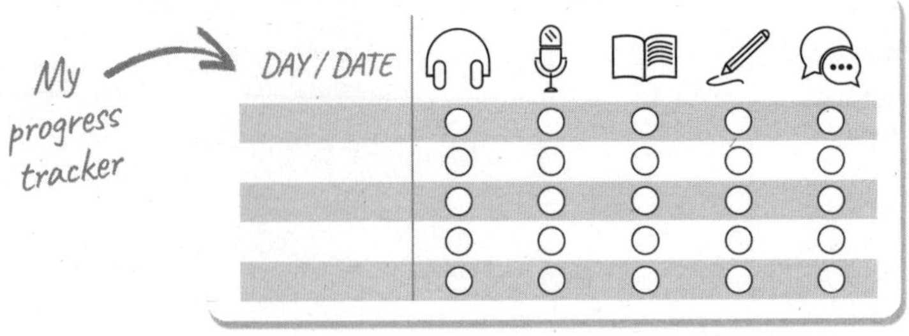

Daily life

Indonesians who have an office **pekerjaan** (*job*) generally work five days a **minggu** (*week*), but exceptions are made on **Jum'at siang** (*Friday afternoon*) when Muslim men attend communal worship at the **masjid** (*mosque*). Going to and from work **setiap** (*every*) day is not a light undertaking in urban Indonesia. Commuters **mendengarkan radio** (*listen to the radio*) not only to keep up with their favorite shows but also to monitor the traffic news. Making an early start is recommended if you have appointments to keep, which can make **makan pagi** (*eating breakfast*) a hurried affair. For city-dwellers, **pulang** (*returning home*) can also take hours. Some busy professionals manage by employing a **pembantu rumah tangga** (*household helper*) to do housework such as **berbelanja** (*shopping*) for groceries and **memasak makan malam** (*cooking dinner*) for the family. The custom in humid and hot Indonesia is to **mandi** (*bathe, shower*) twice a day, once after **bangun** (*waking up*) in the morning and once in the afternoon or evening. Part of the evening may also be spent **menonton televisi** (*watching television*), a popular Indonesian pastime, or helping the children while they **membuat pekerjaan rumah** (*do homework*) before going to **tidur** (*sleep*) at night, perhaps dreaming of the **akhir minggu** (*weekend*).

How would you say *eat lunch* in Indonesian?

Vocabulary builder

04.01 Look at the words and phrases and complete the English translations. Then listen to the recording and imitate the pronunciation of the speakers.

DAYS OF THE WEEK

Senin	*Monday*
Selasa	*Tuesday*
Rabu	*Wednesday*
Kamis	*Thursday*
Jum'at	________
Sabtu	*Saturday*
Minggu	________

When they're not being informal, Indonesians will say **hari Sabtu** or **hari Selasa** instead of only **Sabtu** or **Selasa**.

NUMBERS

In Indonesian, larger numbers come in groups similar to those in English, such as **belasan** (*teens*) and **puluhan** (*tens*).

10 sepuluh	20 dua puluh
11 sebelas	21 dua puluh satu
12 dua belas	22 dua puluh dua
13 tiga belas	23 dua puluh tiga
14 empat belas	24 dua puluh empat
15 lima belas	25 dua puluh lima
16 enam belas	26 dua puluh enam
17 tujuh belas	27 dua puluh tujuh
18 delapan belas	28 dua puluh delapan
19 sembilan belas	29 dua puluh sembilan

_____ tiga puluh

_____ tiga puluh satu

_____ sembilan puluh

_____ sembilan puluh sembilan

NEW EXPRESSIONS

akan	*will, going to, shall*
perusahaan	*company, corporation*
Maaf.	*Sorry.*
Tidak apa-apa.	*It's nothing., No worries.*
seorang	*one person* (classifier)
pegawai negeri	*civil servant*
Kapan	*When* (interrogative)
pada	*at, on, in*
umur	*age*
tahun	*year*

Conversation 1

04.02 *Nani is talking to her colleague Frans.*

1 When is Frans' wife coming home?

Nani	Pak Frans, nanti sore kita akan pergi ke kantor perusahaan IndoTel, ya?
Frans	Hari ini hari apa?
Nani	Hari ini hari Kamis.
Frans	Oh ya. Maaf. Saya sibuk sekali minggu ini. Istri saya sedang bekerja di Lampung.
Nani	Oh, tidak apa-apa. Apa pekerjaan dia?
Frans	Dia seorang pegawai negeri.
Nani	Kapan dia pergi?
Frans	Dia pergi pada hari Selasa. Dia akan pulang pada akhir minggu.
Nani	Siapa memasak di rumah minggu ini?
Frans	Setiap hari pembantu memasak tetapi anak saya juga membantu dia di dapur.
Nani	Oh begitu. Berapa umur anak Pak Frans?
Frans	Dia berumur enam belas tahun.
Nani	Oh ya, Pak Frans sudah makan siang?
Frans	Sudah, Bu. Saya sudah makan siang.
Nani	Baiklah. Sampai nanti!
Frans	Sampai nanti!

sibuk sekali	*very busy*
tetapi	*but*
membantu	*help, assist*
dapur	*kitchen*

2 **Read or listen again and answer the questions.**

- **a** What day is it?
- **b** What does Frans' wife do for a living?
- **c** How old is Frans' child?
- **d** Has Frans had lunch?

3 **Match the questions or statements to the replies.**

a Hari ini hari apa?	**1** Dia pergi pada hari Selasa.
b Sampai nanti!	**2** Tidak apa-apa.
c Maaf.	**3** Sampai nanti!
d Kapan dia pergi?	**4** Hari ini hari Kamis.

4 **Check, then cover up the replies and see if you can say them without looking at the conversation.**

5 **04.03 Now listen to the lines from the conversation and repeat. Then listen to Frans' lines and respond as Nani.**

Language discovery 1

Look at the sentences from the conversation. Put the words in English into Indonesian.

- **a** (*When*) mereka memasak? Mereka memasak (*every*) hari.
- **b** Saya (*will*) mandi sore ini.
- **c** Budi memasak (*dinner*). Saya (*eat dinner*) di rumah dia.
- **d** (*How many*) umur bapak kamu?

1 WHEN

To ask about *when* something happens, Indonesians use the question word **kapan**. In reply, you use the preposition **pada** to mean *on* a certain day or *at/in* a certain time. If the event occurs regularly, use the word **setiap** to mean *each* or *every* particular day or time.

Kapan kamu berbelanja?	*When do you shop?*
Saya berbelanja pada hari Kamis.	*I shop on Thursday.*
Saya berbelanja setiap hari Kamis.	*I shop every Thursday.*

2 FUTURE ACTION

You can indicate future action by stating when the action will happen or by using **akan** (*will, going to*) before the verb.

Saya akan membuat pekerjaan rumah. *I will do homework.*

3 MEALS

By combining **makan** (*eat*) with a time of day, you can form words for **makan pagi** (*breakfast*), **makan siang** (*lunch*), and **makan malam** (*dinner*). You can then use the same words to say *eating breakfast, eating lunch*, and *eating dinner*. It is similar to how the word *lunch* in English can mean both *eating lunch* and the meal itself.

4 AGES

When asking about ages, **berapa** is used because the answer involves a number. In reply, you can omit **tahun** (*year*) if it is clear that you are counting in years.

Berapa umur dia? *What is his age?*
Umur dia dua puluh tahun. *His age is twenty.*

Indonesians also often use the **ber-** verbal prefix to transform the noun **umur** (*age*) into the verb **berumur** (*to be aged*).

Dia berumur dua puluh tahun. *He is twenty.* (lit. *His age is twenty*)

Practice

1 Put the following sentences into Indonesian.
- **a** When do you eat breakfast?
- **b** I will shop today.
- **c** I am sleeping at the hotel on Wednesday night.
- **d** Every Sunday I study Indonesian and cook dinner.

2 Put the following sentences into English.
- **a** Linda akan bangun besok pagi.
- **b** Dia akan pergi ke masjid setiap hari Jum'at.
- **c** Saya akan membuat pekerjaan rumah malam ini.

3 Unscramble the words to make full sentences.
- **a** Frans - memasak? - Pak
- **b** rumah - hari. - siang - di - Jon - setiap - makan
- **c** minggu. - makan - akhir - Ying - pagi - pada
- **d** setiap - memasak - malam. - Budi - malam - makan

4 04.04 Practice asking and answering questions about your age and the ages of your family members.

Pronunciation

04.05 In Indonesian, the punctuation mark ' indicates a glottal stop. When two identical vowels are together, such as *aa*, there is also a glottal stop between them. A glottal stop is a sound some English speakers make in place of the letters *tt* when they pronounce the word *butter*. Listen to how the following words are pronounced and repeat.

1 Jum'at
2 maaf
3 pekerjaan
4 perusahaan

Speaking

04.06 1 Look at Nani's schedule and talk about it in Indonesian.

Monday	shower and go to the office
Tuesday	go home, cook dinner
Wednesday	eat lunch at the office
Thursday	go to the bank, sleep
Friday	eat lunch at my parents' house
Saturday	watch television and bathe
Sunday	study English

2 Now talk about your schedule.

Conversation 2

04.07 *Nani is getting to know Linda, her new neighbor.*

1 What does Linda do?

Nani	Apa pekerjaan Anda?
Linda	Saya seorang insinyur.
Nani	Wah. Di mana Anda bekerja?
Linda	Saya bekerja di sebuah perusahaan asing.
Nani	Berapa umur Anda?
Linda	Umur saya dua puluh delapan tahun.
Nani	Oh begitu. Maaf, ya? Saya harus pergi tidur.
Linda	Tidak apa-apa. Selamat tidur.

Wah	(expression of awe)
insinyur	*engineer*
sebuah	*one thing* (classifier)
asing	*foreign*

Indonesians may add **ya?** to the end of sentences simply to add gentleness to their speech. Unlike the addition of *yes?* at the end of a sentence in English, it is not always a way of asking for confirmation.

2 Read or listen again and answer the following questions.

a Where does Linda work?
b How old is Linda?
c What must Nani do?
d What do you think *Selamat tidur* means?

3 Match the Indonesian to the English.

a sebuah perusahaan	**1** *an employee*
b seorang pegawai	**2** *a company*
c seorang insinyur	**3** *a helper*
d seorang pembantu	**4** *an engineer*

4 4.08 Now listen to the lines from the conversation and repeat. Be sure to pay attention to the pronunciation.

Language discovery 2

Put the following sentences from the conversation into English.

a Saya bekerja di sebuah perusahaan asing.

b Saya seorang insinyur.

1 COUNTING WITH CLASSIFIERS

In formal Indonesian, nouns are classified according to their type, shape, size, and are counted using their specific classifiers. The word **orang** (*person*), for example, is used as a classifier for people, so **dua orang insinyur** means *two engineers*. Animals are counted in **ekor** and large objects are counted in **buah**. For example, **tiga ekor burung** means *three birds* and **empat buah hotel** means *four hotels*. When there is just one of something, add the prefix **se-** to the beginning of the classifier so that you can say, for example, **seorang anak** (*a child*). In this case, **seorang** translates as *a* or *an*. In informal everyday speech, classifiers are not always used, but you should be aware of their function and try to use them when others do.

2 OCCUPATIONS

Some occupation words in Indonesia look similar to the English, such as **dokter** (*medical doctor*) and **akuntan** (*accountant*), but there are many more that don't. You may have noticed that some can be formed using the prefix **pe-** such as the word **pembantu** (*helper*) to mean a person who **membantu** (*helps*) or **pegawai** (*worker*) to mean someone who is doing **gawai** (*work*).

Practice

1 Complete the phrases using the correct classifiers.

a dua ________ kanguru

b delapan ________ perusahaan

c enam ________ pegawai

d se________ rumah tangga

2 04.09 Practice asking and answering questions about your occupation.

Listening

1 04.10 Listen to the recording. Match the day of the week to the activity Budi did on that day.

pada Kamis malam	*on Thursday evening*

a Monday	**1** went to the bank
b Tuesday	**2** cooked in the kitchen
c Wednesday	**3** went to the mosque
d Thursday	**4** ate lunch at the office
e Friday	**5** called Jon
f Saturday	**6** helped the children do their homework
g Sunday	**7** woke up and ate breakfast at home

2 04.11 Read the questions below and prepare your own responses. Then, listen and respond. Do this as many times as you need to for it to become second nature.

Berapa umur Anda?

Umur saya empat puluh lima tahun.

a Hari ini hari apa?
b Kapan Anda mendengarkan radio?
c Apa pekerjaan Anda?

Reading and writing

1 Paul is currently working in Indonesia. He writes a post on an Indonesian internet forum. Read Paul's post and check the glossary if there are words you don't know.

Halo teman-teman! Saya Paul. Saya berumur tiga puluh tujuh tahun. Saya seorang guru bahasa Inggris. Saya sedang bekerja di Surabaya, dan istri saya sedang bekerja di Palembang. Dia sibuk sekali. Saya mengajar di sekolah setiap hari Senin, Selasa, dan Rabu. Pada hari Kamis, saya makan siang di hotel dan menonton film di bioskop. Pada hari Jum'at, istri saya sampai di Surabaya, dan kami makan malam di rumah Pak Sardi, tetangga kami, malam itu. Saya akan menonton televisi dan belajar bahasa Indonesia pada akhir minggu. Saya sudah mulai mengerti bahasa Indonesia tetapi saya masih harus belajar. Baiklah, saya akan tidur sekarang. Selamat malam!

2 Write a post like Paul's about your recent daily activities using what you know.

Go further

As you know, Indonesian revolves around root words you can build on by adding affixes. By adding **pe-** and **-an** to the word **kerja** (*to work*), you form the noun **pekerjaan** (*job*).

Here are **pekerjaan-pekerjaan** (*jobs*) you might come across:

bidan	*midwife*
ibu rumah tangga	*homemaker, housewife*
ilmuwan	*scientist*
karyawan swasta	*private-sector employee*
kuli	*unskilled laborer*
pekerja LSM	*NGO worker*
pelajar	*student*
pelukis	*painter*
penari	*dancer*
peneliti	*researcher*
pengajar	*educator*
perawat	*nurse*
tukang	*skilled laborer, handyperson*
wartawan	*journalist*

An affix attached to the end of a word is a suffix. The suffix **-wan** (masculine) and **-wati** (feminine) means someone who is knowledgeable and professional in a particular field.

If you are retired you can say you are a **pensiunan** (*retiree*) or that you **sudah pensiun** (*already retired*).

1 Match the occupations to the actions. Complete the English translations of the actions.

a peneliti	**1** melukis ________
b pelajar	**2** menari ________
c pelukis	**3** meneliti ________
d penari	**4** belajar ________

2 04.12 Read the questions below and prepare your own reponses. Then, listen and respond in real time. Do this as many times as you need to for it to become second nature.

a Apa pekerjaan Isaac Newton?

b Apa pekerjaan Florence Nightingale?

Test yourself

1 Put the words in English into Indonesian.
  - **a** (*When*) kamu mandi?
  - **b** Aku mendengarkan radio (*every Tuesday night*).
  - **c** Aku menonton televisi (*at the weekend*).
  - **d** Aku pergi ke kantor (*on Monday*).

2 Give the English for the following.
  - **a** Saya akan membantu ibu berbelanja pada hari Sabtu.
  - **b** Mereka akan memasak besok malam.
  - **c** Saya akan pergi ke gereja pada hari Minggu.

3 Use the words in the box to recreate the phrases below.

makan, makan, makan, memasak, malam, siang, pagi

  - **a** cook breakfast
  - **b** eat lunch
  - **c** dinner

4 Match the Indonesian to the English.

a Umur dia lima belas tahun.	**1** He is seventy years old.
b Dia berumur tiga puluh tahun.	**2** He is fifteen years old.
c Umur dia tujuh puluh tahun.	**3** She is thirty years old.

5 Put the following words into Indonesian.
  - **a** eight children
  - **b** nineteen civil servants
  - **c** twenty-five television sets
  - **d** an NGO worker

6 Choose the correct word.
  - **a** Apa *pekerjaan / bekerja* Anda?
  - **b** Di mana beliau *bekerja / pekerja*?
  - **c** Dia seorang *belajar / pelajar*.

SELF CHECK

	I CAN . . .
○	. . . talk about daily activities.
○	. . . use the days of the week to talk about an event or a habit.
○	. . . talk about what I and others do for a living.
○	. . . ask for and give ages.
○	. . . count people, animals, and large objects.

5

In this unit, you will learn how to:

» describe and ask for things.
» ask and understand how much things cost.
» pay for your shopping and receive change.
» make and understand requests.
» obtain basic information from adverts.

Berapa harganya?

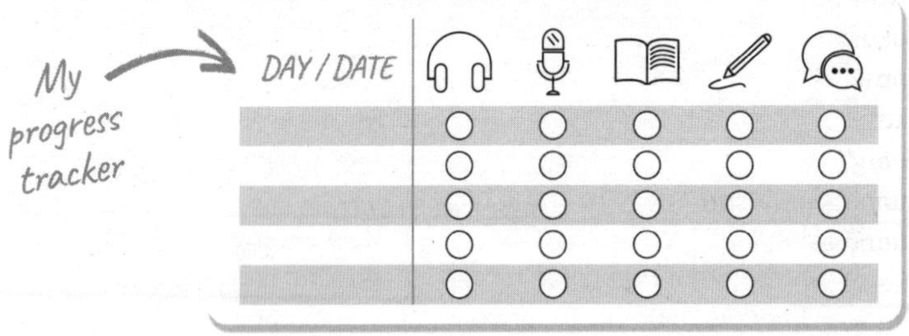

Shopping

Whether you need to replace a pair of **sepatu** (*shoes*) or are looking for a **kain tradisional** (*traditional cloth*) such as the painted and patterned batik, in Indonesia there is a shopping experience to suit any budget. A medium-sized city will have at least one **mal** (*mall*) or **pusat perbelanjaan** (*shopping center*) where you can find many stores, the **pasar swalayan** (*supermarket*), and the department store or **toserba**, which is short for **toko serba ada** (*store that has various things*). Every community in Indonesia will also have its own traditional **pasar** (*market*), where you can buy your **belanjaan sehari-hari** (*everyday shopping*), some **elektronik** (*electronics*), and **pakaian** (*clothes*). You do not need to go far, though, to buy necessities such as **pasta gigi** (*toothpaste*) or **baterai** (*batteries*) because they are commonly available at the **warung** (*street stall*), which you can find at the bottom of the neighborhood **ruko** (*shophouse*) or at a little roadside hut. When visiting Indonesia on holiday, do seek out the specialized markets, such as the **pasar seni** (*craft and art market*), to find a unique **oleh-oleh** (*souvenir*). With some

Indonesian rupiah in hand, you can **beli** (*buy*) just about anything you **suka** (*like*) in Indonesia.

How would you say *batik shop* in Indonesian?

Vocabulary builder

1 05.01 Look at the words and phrases and complete the English translations. Then listen to the recording and imitate the pronunciation of the speakers.

SHOPPING

harga	*price*
warna	*color*
ukuran	*size*
pas	*to fit, accurate, exactly*
kasir	*cashier, till* (coll.)
uang	*money* (also *notes* and *coins*)
uang kembalian	*change*
uang tunai	*cash*
kartu kredit	____________
diskon	____________

ADJECTIVES

mahal	*expensive*
murah	*cheap*
besar	*large*
kecil	*small*
panjang	*long*
pendek	*short*

NEW EXPRESSIONS

cari	*look for, search for*
boleh	*may, to be allowed to*
lihat	*see, look at*
yang	*that, which, that which*
Yang mana?	*Which one/ones?*
ada	*there is/are, has/have, to be available*
coba	*try*
tunggu sebentar	*wait a moment*
ambil	*take*

bayar	*pay*
kalau	*if, when*
mau	*want*
Kembali.	*(Thanks) in return./You're welcome.*

The response **kembali** is short for **terima kasih kembali** meaning *thank you in return.*

NUMBERS

In Indonesian, the **se-** prefix often takes the place of **satu** (*one*).

100	**seratus**	500	**lima ratus**
1,000	**seribu**	5,000	**lima ribu**
10,000	**sepuluh ribu**	50,000	**lima puluh ribu**
100,000	**seratus ribu**	500,000	**lima ratus ribu**
1,000,000	**sejuta** *or* **satu juta**	5,000,000	**lima juta**

Prices of everyday goods in Indonesian rupiah run into the tens and hundreds of thousands. Being familiar with large numbers is a necessity, especially if you plan to shop at markets or road stalls where many items do not have a price sticker.

QUALIFIERS

kurang	*not quite, less*
lebih	*more*
paling	*most*
terlalu	*too, overly*

COLORS

merah	*red*	**biru**	*blue*
kuning	*yellow*	**hijau**	*green*
putih	*white*	**hitam**	*black*
cokelat	*brown*	**abu-abu**	*gray*

When referring to a color, Indonesians will say, for example, **warna putih** instead of only **putih** (*white*).

CLOTHING

kaos	*T-shirt*	**kemeja**	*shirt*
celana panjang	*trousers*	**rok**	*skirt*
jas	*blazer, coat*	**dasi**	*tie*
baju dalam	*underclothes*	**topi**	*hat*
kaos kaki	*socks*	**sandal**	*sandals*

Remember, you don't need to pluralize items that usually come in pairs, such as **sandal** (*sandals*), unless you're talking about many pairs of them.

2 05.02 **Listen to the numbers and useful words and imitate the pronunciation of the speakers.**

Conversation 1

05.03 *Tono is a teenager shopping at a department store and Mokhtar is a sales attendant who is helping him.*

1 How much are the black shoes?

Mokhtar Kamu cari apa?
Tono Aku cari sepatu. Aku boleh lihat yang itu?
Mokhtar Yang mana?
Tono Yang biru.
[*Mokhtar gives Tono the shoes Tono pointed to.*]
Tono Berapa harganya?
Mokhtar Harganya tiga ratus ribu rupiah.
Tono Itu terlalu mahal. Ada sepatu yang lebih murah?
Mokhtar Ada. Yang hitam dua ratus ribu rupiah.
Tono Yang hitam sepatu yang paling murah?
Mokhtar Ya. Yang paling murah. Cobalah.
[*Tono tries on the shoes.*]
Tono Yang ini kurang pas. Yang ini terlalu kecil.
Mokhtar Berapa ukuranmu?
Tono Ukuranku empat puluh satu.
Mokhtar Tolong tunggu sebentar. Saya cari ukuranmu.
[*Mokhtar returns with the shoes and Tono tries them on.*]
Tono Ya. Yang ini pas. Aku ambil yang ini.
Mokhtar Silakan bayar di kasir.
Tono Aku boleh bayar dengan kartu kredit?
Mokhtar Boleh, tetapi hari ini kalau kamu bayar tunai, ada diskon sepuluh persen.

2 Find the expressions in the conversation that mean:

a Try (them on). ____________
b Please wait a moment. ____________
c Please pay at the till. ____________

3 **Read or listen again and answer the questions.**

a What color are the cheapest shoes?

b What is Tono's shoe size?

c How can Tono qualify for the ten percent discount?

4 **05.04 Now listen to the lines from the conversation and repeat. Be sure to pay attention to the pronunciation.**

Language discovery 1

Look at the sentences from the conversation. Put the words in English into Indonesian.

a Aku boleh lihat (*those ones*)? Yang mana? (*The blue ones.*)

b (*Please*) tunggu sebentar. (*Please*) bayar di kasir.

c Ada (*cheaper shoes*)?

d Berapa (*your size*)? (*My size*) empat puluh satu.

e Berapa (*its price*)?

1 SINGLING OUT ITEMS USING *YANG*

To single out items, you can use the word **yang** (*that, which*) in several ways. When you say **topi yang biru**, you're talking about *the hat that is blue* and not any other hat. You don't always need to use the noun **topi** (*hat*) either. You can simply say **yang biru** (*the blue one*). Similarly, instead of saying **topi yang itu** (*that hat*), you can say **yang itu** (*that one*). If you need clarification when others are pointing at items, ask **Yang mana?** (*Which one?*)

Note that since in the Indonesian **yang ini** (*this one*) does not actually describe the number of items present, it can also mean *these ones*. Similarly, **yang biru** can be either *the blue one* or *the blue ones*.

2 MAKING REQUESTS OR SUGGESTIONS

When requesting or suggesting an action, you can simply use the verb. Sometimes **-lah** is added to the verb for emphasis.

Coba sepatu itu. Cobalah sepatu itu.

Try (on) those shoes. Do try (on) those shoes.

To be more polite, you can use the word **silakan** (*please, go ahead*) when the action will benefit the person to whom the action is suggested. However, you should use the word **tolong** (*please, help*) when the action you request will be mutually beneficial or beneficial to you.

Silakan bayar di kasir.

Please (for your convenience) pay at the till.

Tolong tunggu sebentar. Saya cari ukuranmu.

Please wait a moment (for me). I will look for your size.

3 QUALIFYING DESCRIPTIONS

When you want to describe something as being **terlalu kecil** (*too small*) or **kurang kecil** (*not small enough*), or if you want to say you are looking for something **lebih kecil** (*smaller*) or for **paling kecil** (*the smallest*) of its kind, place the qualifier before the adjective.

Ini kecil. Ini kurang kecil. Ini terlalu kecil.

This is small. This is not small enough. This is too small.

The word **yang** is necessary when you're describing a noun, for example **sepatu yang lebih murah** (*the cheaper shoes*). When the noun, in this case **sepatu** (*shoes*), is already known, you can simply say **yang lebih murah** to mean *the cheaper ones*.

4 ATTACHED POSSESSIVE PRONOUNS

In Indonesian, possessive pronouns such as **aku** (*my*), **kamu** (*your*), **dia** (*his/her*), and **mereka** (*their*) are often attached to the noun in the form of suffixes such as **-ku** (*my*), **-mu** (*your*), and **-nya** (*his/her, their*).

Therefore, **ukuran aku** becomes **ukuranku** (*my size*), **ukuran kamu** becomes **ukuranmu** (*your size*) and **ukuran dia** or **ukuran mereka** becomes **ukurannya** (*his/her size, their size*). In this way, an inanimate object such as an item for sale can also be treated as possessive, for example **harganya** (*its price*).

When talking about a noun phrase, such as **ukuran celana** (*trouser size*), you attach the pronoun to the end of the phrase.

Berapa ukuran celanamu?

What is your trouser size?

5 PRICE

When you ask how much something is, you are asking for **harganya** (*its price*). Since the answer involves a number, you should use the question word **berapa**. In everyday speech it is not always necessary to include the currency.

Berapa harganya? Harganya lima puluh ribu rupiah.

What is its price? Its price is fifty thousand rupiah.

Berapa harga yang itu? Sepuluh ribu.

What is that one's price? Ten thousand.

Practice

1 Put the following sentences into Indonesian.

a Which one is the cheaper one?

b I'm taking that one.

c Try this blazer.

2 Put the words in English into Indonesian.

a (*Please, help*) cari ukuran saya.

b (*Please, go ahead*) bayar dengan kartu kredit.

3 Put the following sentences into English.

a Celana pendek itu terlalu besar.

b Kaos kaki ini kurang panjang.

c Terima kasih! Ukurannya pas.

4 Replace the pronouns with attached pronouns.

a Aku tidak tahu ukuran aku.

b Ukuran kemeja saya empat belas.

c Rok dia coklat dan rok kamu abu-abu.

5 05.05 Practice asking and telling others about how much things cost in Indonesian rupiah.

Pronunciation

05.06 The Indonesian consonant *ny* is used frequently and unlike in English, it can also be found at the beginning of words and immediately after other consonants. Listen to how the following words are pronounced and repeat.

> Try to pronounce the English words *canyon* and *onion* while paying attention to the *ny* sound you are making.

1 harganya

2 ukurannya

3 pakaiannya

4 nyamuk

Speaking

05.07 Read the questions below and prepare your own responses. Then, listen and respond. Do this as many times as you need to for it to become second nature.

a Di mana kamu berbelanja?

b Kalau di Indonesia, kamu berbelanja di ruko?

c Berapa ukuranmu?

Conversation 2

05.08 *Linda goes to a street stall to shop.*

Linda	Selamat siang, Pak.
Penjual	Selamat siang. Ibu mau beli apa?
Linda	Saya mau beli sikat gigi, Pak.
Penjual	Ibu suka warna apa?
Linda	Saya suka warna hijau muda dan warna biru tua.
[*The vendor shows Linda the goods.*]	
Penjual	Ini, Bu. Ibu mau yang mana?
Linda	Saya ambil yang biru tua. Berapa harganya?
Penjual	Sepuluh ribu saja. Ibu mau beli pasta gigi juga?
Linda	Tidak. Terima kasih. Saya tidak mau beli pasta gigi hari ini.
Penjual	Oh ya. Tidak apa-apa.
Linda	Saya tidak ada uang pas. Saya ada uang dua puluh ribu saja. Ada uang kembalian?
Penjual	Ada. Ini kembalian Ibu. Sepuluh ribu pas.
Linda	Terima kasih.
Penjual	Kembali.

penjual	*vendor, seller*
sikat	*brush*
suka	*like* (v.)
saja	*merely, only*

1 What does Linda want to buy?

2 Match the Indonesian to the English.

a yang biru tua	**1** *ten thousand exactly*
b uang dua puluh ribu	**2** *the dark blue one*
c sepuluh ribu pas	**3** *change*
d uang kembalian	**4** *a twenty-thousand rupiah note*

3 Check, then cover up your answers and see if you can say them without looking at the conversation.

4 Read or listen again and answer the following questions.

a What colors did Linda say she likes?

b What else did the stall vendor offer Linda?

c What was the denomination of the bill that Linda used to pay?

d Did the vendor have change?

5 05.09 Now listen to the lines from the conversation and repeat. Then listen to the vendor's lines and respond as Linda.

Language discovery 2

Look at the sentences from the conversation. Put the words in English into Indonesian.

a Ibu (*want to buy*) apa?

b Saya (*have*) uang dua puluh ribu. (*Is there*) uang kembalian?

c Saya suka warna (*light green*) dan (*deep blue*).

1 VERB COMBINATIONS

When you need to combine verbs to say, for example, that you *want to buy* something, you simply put **mau** (*want*) and **beli** (*buy*) together to make **mau beli.** When you negate it, you should place **tidak** before the combination.

2 THE VERB *ADA*

The verb **ada** can mean *there is* or *here are.*

Ada toko komputer di mal itu.	*There is a computer store in that shopping mall.*

Colloquially, you can also use it to mean *to have.*

Saya ada uang pas.	*I have exact change.*

It can also mean *to be available.*

Kemeja yang putih masih ada.	*The white shirt is still available.*

3 DARKER AND LIGHTER COLORS

Consider how the color of a plant's leaves grows into a deeper green as it ages throughout the growing season. When you want to talk about a darker version of a color, you can use the word **tua** to mean *dark* or *deep* so that, for example, **merah tua** is *dark red* or *deep red*. To talk about a lighter version of a color, you can use the word **muda** to mean *light* so that, for example, **merah muda** is *light red* or *pink*.

Practice

1 **Put the words in English into Indonesian.**
   - **a** Saya (*may see*) dasi (*that is yellow*)?
   - **b** Dia (*want to go*) ke (*street stall*) dan beli baterai.

2 **Put the following sentences into English.**
   - **a** Maaf. Saya tidak ada uang pas.
   - **b** Sandal itu masih ada, Pak, dan ada diskon dua puluh persen!

3 **05.10 Practice describing the colors of things.**

Sandal saya putih.
Kaos saya abu-abu muda....

Listening

dijual	*for sale* (lit. *being sold*)
hubungi	*contact* (v.)
sepasang	*a pair of*
setengah	*half*

1 05.11 **Maya is looking at the classifieds in the paper whilst eating breakfast with her husband Slamet. Listen to the dialogue and answer the following questions.**

a Is the house large or small?

b Why are they interested in the house?

c How much is the house?

2 05.12 **Benny is at the market. Listen to the dialogue and complete the sentences in the story.**

Benny mau membeli sepasang sendal _______. Ukurannya _______. _______ ukurannya di pasar. Sekarang dia akan coba pergi ke _______ di mana sendal itu juga _______. Kalau tidak ada juga di _______, Benny harus pergi ke _______.

The word **dijual** (*to be sold*) comes from the prefix **di-** and the word **jual** (*to sell*). In Indonesia, it is the most common way to title for sale listings.

Reading and writing

1 Whose advert has Amelia responded to?

In Indonesia, contactless card payment is available. You will see it written in English or as **tanpa sentuh** meaning *without touch*.

rukopedia Home Profile Find People Settings Help

DIJUAL sepatu anak-anak. Warna kuning, hijau, dan merah masih ada. Murah dan bagus! Hubungi Ira 016.726.0924

DIJUAL murah! Barang-barang elektronik: komputer, HP, telepon, baterai! Boleh bayar dengan kartu kredit tanpa sentuh. Hubungi Santoso di Toko Tugu 0811.3038.7712

Halo. Saya lihat iklan Anda. Saya mau sepasang sepatu anak-anak yang kuning dan sepasang yang merah. Ukuran anak saya 3 1/2. Kalau ukuran dan warna itu masih ada, tolong hubungi saya di 0811.6690.0925. Amelia

2 Imagine you are responding to one of the above adverts. Write your reply. Don't forget to give your contact details.

Go further

In Indonesian, composing large numbers is done in a similar way to how it is done in English. You start with the largest group, for example the **jutaan** (*millions*), and move to the second largest, for example the **ribuan** (*thousands*), then to the **ratusan** (*hundreds*) and to the tens, and so on.

2015 = 2,000 + 15
dua ribu lima belas
two thousand (and) fifteen
23,450 = 23,000 + 400 + 50
dua puluh tiga ribu empat ratus lima puluh
twenty-three thousand, four hundred (and) fifty
2,630,500 = 2,000,000 + 630,000 + 500
dua juta enam ratus tiga puluh ribu lima ratus
two million, six hundred (and) thirty thousand, (and) five hundred

1 Put the following amounts of money into Indonesian.

- **a** 950 rupiah
- **b** 4,200 rupiah
- **c** 12,900 rupiah
- **d** 750,000 rupiah
- **e** 1,625,000 rupiah

2 Match the Indonesian to the English.

a apotek	**1** *electronics store*
b toko elektronik	**2** *copy store*
c pasar seni	**3** *bookstore*
d toko fotokopi	**4** *arts and crafts market*
e toko buku	**5** *pharmacy*

3 05.13 Read the questions below and prepare your own responses. Then, listen and respond in real time. Do this as many times as you need to for it to become second nature.

- **a** Di mana Anda mau membeli oleh-oleh dari Indonesia?
- **b** Anda paling suka warna apa?
- **c** Berapa harga belanjaan sehari-hari Anda?
- **d** Di kota Anda, di mana aspirin dijual?

Test yourself

1 Put the words in English into Indonesian.

- **a** (*Which one*) kamu mau lihat?
- **b** Saya boleh lihat (*that one*)?
- **c** Saya mau membeli (*this one*).

2 Complete the sentences to make polite requests.

- **a** _______ bayar dengan uang pas. *(for your/mutual benefit)*
- **b** _______ coba yang Anda suka. *(for the other person's benefit)*

3 Match the Indonesian to the English.

a kurang murah	**1** *too large*
b paling kecil	**2** *not cheap enough*
c terlalu besar	**3** *smallest*

4 Put the following sentences into English.

- **a** Ini bukan ukuranku.
- **b** Ukuranmu tujuh setengah.
- **c** Ukurannya terlalu kecil.

5 Unscramble the words to make full sentences.
  a coklat - yang - harga - pendek - Berapa - rok ?
  b mahal. - terlalu - tidak - Harganya
6 Choose the correct phrase.
  a Saya *mau ke pergi* / *mau pergi* ke pasar seni.
  b Saya *boleh coba* / *boleh ke coba* celana panjang itu?
7 Insert the word **ada** into the sentences to correct them.
  a Tidak baju dalam di toko ini.
  b Kami kain-kain tradisional.
8 Choose the correct English translation.
  a merah muda *pink* / *dark red*
  b hijau tua *light green* / *dark green*.

SELF CHECK

I CAN . . .
. . . describe and ask for things.
. . . ask and understand how much things cost.
. . . pay for my shopping and receive change.
. . . make and understand requests.
. . . obtain basic information from adverts.

6

In this unit, you will learn how to:

» talk about types of accommodation.
» express your preferences and make reservations.
» use the months of the year to talk about dates.
» ask for and give addresses.
» ask for, give, and understand Indonesian spelling.

Anda menginap di mana?

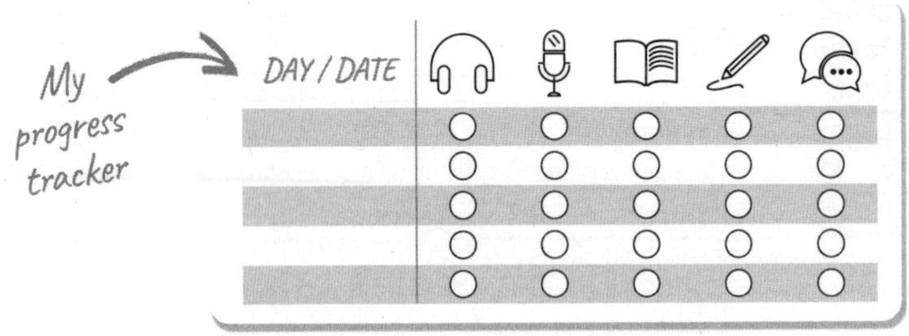

Accommodation

Finding **akomodasi** (*accommodation*) in Indonesia that offers what you **perlu** (*need*) and like, such as **AC** (*air conditioning*) or internet access, will be easy. If you prefer staying in hotels, you can choose a **hotel berbintang** (*star-rated hotel*) or a **hotel melati** (*budget hotel*), where your room will come with fewer or more modest **fasilitas** (*amenities*). With Indonesia being a tropical country, not all accommodations feature **air panas** (*hot water*). Bathrooms may also come with only a **bak mandi** (*bathtub*) and a **gayung** (*dipper*) that you use to scoop water out of the tub to wash yourself instead of a **pancuran mandi** (*shower*). In smaller cities, you can **menginap** (*stay overnight*) at the more intimate and often family-run **losmen** (*guesthouses*). If you find yourself in a town or **desa** (*village*) where there is no **penginapan** (*commercially run accommodation*), you're likely to meet locals who will want to host you as their **tamu** (*guest*). When staying for more than a **bulan** (*month*), you can consider **menyewa** (*renting*) a residence of your own or a **kamar kos** (*bedsit*), where you would live with an Indonesian family or in a specially built **rumah kos** (*boarding house*), as Indonesian students and young professionals often do.

How would you say *I need hot water amenities* in Indonesian?

Vocabulary builder

06.01 Look at the words and phrases and complete the English translations. Then listen to the recording and imitate the pronunciation of the speakers.

ACCOMMODATION

kamar singel	*single room*
kamar dobel	________ *room*
kamar mandi	*bathroom*
kamar mandi dalam	*en-suite bathroom*
tarif	*rate, fee, fare*
per malam, semalam	________, *a night*
memesan	*book* (v.), *order* (v.)
reservasi, pemesanan	*reservation*
konfirmasi	________

MONTHS OF THE YEAR

Januari	*January*
Februari	*February*
Maret	*March*
April	*April*
Mei	*May*
Juni	*June*
Juli	*July*
Agustus	*August*
September	*September*
Oktober	*October*
November, Nopember	*November*
Desember	*December*

NEW EXPRESSIONS

tanggal	*date*
untuk	*for, for the purpose of*

lebih ... daripada ...	*more ... than ...*
atau	*or*
dalam	*inside, within, in*
hanya	*only*
lahir	*to be born*

Conversation 1

06.02 *Linda calls a guesthouse to book a room.*

1 When does Linda want to stay at the guesthouse?

The pronunciation of **AC** is a mix of English and Indonesian.

Shinta	Halo. Losmen Ratu. Ini Shinta. Bisa saya bantu?
Linda	Halo. Ini Linda Curtis. Saya mencari akomodasi untuk akhir bulan Mei.
Shinta	Pada tanggal berapa Anda mau menginap?
Linda	Saya mau menginap dari tanggal tiga puluh Mei sampai tanggal dua Juni. Saya perlu satu kamar.
Shinta	Kami ada kamar kosong untuk tanggal-tanggal tersebut. Untuk berapa orang tamu?
Linda	Untuk dua orang tamu. Saya dan suami saya.
Shinta	Anda mau kamar ber-AC atau tanpa AC?
Linda	Saya lebih suka kamar ber-AC daripada kamar tanpa AC. Saya kurang suka tidur tanpa AC.
Shinta	Kami ada satu kamar dobel ber-AC dengan kamar mandi di dalam.
Linda	Ada pancuran mandi di dalam kamar mandinya?
Shinta	Maaf. Tidak ada. Hanya ada bak mandi.
Linda	Tidak apa-apa. Apakah ada fasilitas internet?
Shinta	Ya. Ada.
Linda	Berapa tarif kamar per malam?
Shinta	Tarifnya semalam seratus tiga puluh ribu rupiah.
Linda	Baiklah. Saya mau memesan kamar itu.

mencari	*look for, search for*
kosong	*empty*
tersebut	*mentioned, said*
tanpa	*without, lacking*

2 **Find the expressions in the conversation that mean:**

a Can I help (you)? ________

b There isn't. ________

c What is the room rate per night? ________

3 **Read or listen again and answer the questions.**

a Who will be traveling with Linda?

b What are the features of the bathroom?

c How much does the room cost?

4 **06.03 Now listen to the lines from the conversation and repeat. Be sure to pay attention to the pronunciation.**

Language discovery 1

Look at the sentences from the conversation. Put the words in English into Indonesian.

a Saya (*prefer*) hotel berbintang (*instead of*) hotel melati.

b Saya (*do not quite*) suka mandi dengan gayung.

c Dari (*what date*) dia menginap? Dari (*May 30*).

1 EXPRESSING PREFERENCE

You've seen the qualifier **lebih** (*more*) used on its own, but it can also be used with **daripada** (*than*) to explicitly compare one thing with another.

Kamar dobel lebih mahal daripada kamar singel.

A double room is more expensive than a single room.

Using **lebih** (*more*) to say you **suka** (*like*) something more than another thing is an easy way to express your preference.

Saya lebih suka bulan Juni daripada bulan Juli.

I like June more than I like July. I prefer June instead of July.

Saya lebih suka bulan Oktober. *I prefer October.*

2 EXPRESSING DISLIKE

When you want to show dislike, you combine the verb **suka** (*like*) with **tidak** (*not*) to say you **tidak suka** (*do not like*) something. However, Indonesians often prefer to say they merely **kurang suka** (*do not quite like*) something, which is more polite.

Saya kurang suka menginap di rumah mereka.

(lit.) *I do not quite like staying overnight at their house.*

3 THE DATE

When stating a *date*, you'll need to preface it with the word **tanggal**. You should use **pada** when an event happens *on* a particular date and **berapa** as a question word.

Saya menginap di kota Bogor pada tanggal 31 Mei.

I stayed overnight in the city of Bogor on May 31.

Hari ini tanggal berapa? Hari ini tanggal 24 Desember.

What date is it today? Today is the December 24.

As in English, the year is placed at the end of the date, for example **tanggal 24 Desember 2025**. You should say **tahun 2025** if you need to talk about *the year 2025* on its own.

Practice

1 Put the following sentences into Indonesian.

- **a** They prefer a guesthouse instead of a star-rated hotel.
- **b** I prefer a bathroom with hot water amenities.
- **c** She prefers renting a bedsit.

2 Put the following sentences into English.

- **a** Maaf. Saya kurang suka kamar ini.
- **b** Tamu-tamu tidak suka hotel itu.
- **c** Mereka kurang suka tinggal di rumah kos.

3 06.04 Practice asking and telling people what date it is today.

Hari ini tanggal berapa?

Hari ini tanggal 19 Oktober.

Pronunciation

06.05 Listen to how the alphabet is pronounced so you can spell it as an Indonesian speaker. Do this as many times as you need to for it to become second nature.

Speaking

06.06 Look at the schedule, read the questions, and make the reservations. Then, listen and respond in real time.

Di mana Anda mau menginap?

Kapan Anda mau menginap?

Anda perlu berapa kamar?

Untuk berapa orang tamu?

> Recall that when someone is speaking to you, words such as **Anda** (*you, your*) may be replaced by your name.

Conversation 2

06.07 *Shinta and Linda are still on the phone while Shinta makes Linda's reservation at the guesthouse.*

1 What are the details of Linda's reservation?

Shinta	Anda bisa mengeja nama Anda?
Linda	Ya. L—I—N—D—A C—U—R—T—I—S.
Shinta	Terima kasih. Ya, sekarang Ibu Linda sudah ada reservasi di losmen kami dari tanggal tiga puluh Mei sampai tanggal dua Juni. Kamar dobel ber-AC dengan kamar mandi dalam dan fasilitas internet. Betul, Bu?
Linda	Betul. Terima kasih.
Shinta	Kembali. Ibu sudah ada alamat kami?
Linda	Belum. Di mana alamatnya?
Shinta	Alamatnya Jalan Lumumba nomor tiga puluh lima.
Linda	Shinta bisa mengeja nama jalannya?
Shinta	Bisa. L—U—M—U—M—B—A.
Linda	Terima kasih, Shinta.

mengeja	*spell* (v.)
betul	*correct*
alamat	*address*
Jalan	*Street, Road*

2 **Match the questions or statements to the replies.**

a Betul, Bu?	**1** Alamatnya Jalan Lumumba.
b Di mana alamatnya?	**2** Belum.
c Terima kasih.	**3** Betul.
d Ibu sudah ada alamatnya?	**4** Kembali.

3 **Check, then cover up your answers and see if you can say them without looking at the conversation.**

4 **Read or listen again and answer the following questions.**

a What did Shinta ask Linda to do?

b Did Linda have the address of the guesthouse?

c What is the address?

5 **06.08 Now listen to the lines from the conversation and repeat. Then listen to Linda's lines and respond as Shinta.**

Language discovery 2

1 **Refer to the conversation and match the Indonesian to the English.**

a alamatnya	**1** *the street name*
b nama jalannya	**2** *the address*

2 **Unscramble the words to make full sentences using the conversation as a model.**

a alamatnya? - mana - Di

b Lumumba - nomor - puluh - Jalan - Alamatnya - lima. - tiga

1 THE –NYA SUFFIX ACTING AS *THE*

When discussing a particular thing or person, Indonesians add the suffix **-nya** to the noun instead of continually describing *the* thing or person they are talking about. In Conversation 2, it was understood that **alamatnya** (*the address*) was that of the guesthouse. When Linda asked Shinta to spell **nama jalannya** (*the street name*), it was understood that Linda was referring to the street in the address Shinta just gave her.

2 ASKING FOR AND GIVING AN ADDRESS

An address is treated as a location in Indonesian so you need to use **di mana** (*where*) instead of the question word **apa** when asking someone *what* the address is. In an Indonesian address, the street name comes before the house number.

Di mana alamatmu?	*What is your address?*
Alamatku Jalan Pattimura nomor dua belas.	*My address is Pattimura Street No. 12.*

Practice

1 **Put the following questions into Indonesian using the -nya suffix.**
   - **a** Where is the bathroom?
   - **b** Who is the new guest?
   - **c** What is the address?

2 **06.09 Practice asking and answering questions about your address.**

Di mana alamat Anda?

Alamat saya Jalan Geelong nomor tiga belas.

Listening

memberikan ... kepada ...	*give (something) to (someone)*
selama	*for a duration of*
termasuk	*included*

1 **06.10 Listen to the voicemail message left for Jon Curtis by a Hotel Ambarawa staff member and answer the following questions.**
   - **a** When is Jon going to stay at Hotel Ambarawa?
   - **b** How many nights is the reservation for?
   - **c** How much is the room per night in dollars?
   - **d** What is included in the price of the room?

2 **06.11 Listen to the announcement. Write down the dates in Indonesian, matching them with the destinations.**

Surabaya	Ambon	Manado
Semarang	Medan	Batam
Padang	Jakarta	Makassar

Reading and writing

1 Read the booking confirmation email.

New message

Hotel Arjuna

Yth. Ibu Taraji

JL Kintamani No. 14, Depok 16424

Tel. (021)650-0592

Dengan ini kami memberikan konfirmasi pemesanan kamar Anda. Anda menginap selama tiga malam dari tanggal 21 Mei. Satu kamar dobel tanpa AC dengan kamar mandi dalam. Tarif kamar semalam delapan puluh lima dolar, termasuk makan pagi.

Hormat saya,

Irwan Sudibyo

Yth. is short for **Yang Terhormat** (*Whom is most respected*), a standard way of addressing others in Indonesian business correspondence.

2 Complete the hotel registration form for Taraji. Then, practice completing the form with your own details.

Hotel Arjuna	
a Nama Tamu: _______	**b** _______ Lahir: 17/6/1971
c Alamat: _______	**d** Kota: _______
e Kode Pos: _______	**f** No. Telepon: _______

Go further

When choosing your accommodation, you may have particular **keperluan-keperluan** (*needs*). Here are some accommodation features that you may come across.

1 Match the Indonesian to the English.

a	kamar bebas rokok	**1**	*work desk*
b	tempat tidur ekstra	**2**	*iron and ironing board*
c	ranjang bayi	**3**	*extra bed*
d	brankas	**4**	*disability-friendly room*
e	setrika dan papan setrika	**5**	*hair dryer*
f	meja kerja	**6**	*non-smoking room*
g	pembuat teh dan kopi	**7**	*safe*
h	pengering rambut	**8**	*cot*
i	kamar ramah disabilitas	**9**	*tea and coffee maker*

Earlier, you discovered how the word **dalam** can be used with a currency to mean *in* that currency. It can also be used with a language to mean *in* that language. Whenever you need help, you can ask what something means **dalam bahasa Inggris** (*in English*) or **dalam bahasa Indonesia** (*in Indonesian*).

Apa arti 'kolam renang' dalam bahasa Inggris?

What is the meaning of 'kolam renang' in English?

Artinya 'swimming pool'. *Its meaning is 'swimming pool'.*

2 06.12 Put the following dialogue into Indonesian except for the words in quotations. Then, listen to Jon's lines and respond as if you were Budi.

Jon	*What is the meaning of 'internet gratis' in English?*
Budi	*Its meaning is 'free internet'.*
Jon	*What is the meaning of 'unlimited wifi' in Indonesian?*
Budi	*Its meaning is 'koneksi wifi tanpa batas'.*

3 06.13 Read the questions below and prepare responses that are true for you. Then, listen and respond in real time. Do this as many times as you need to for it to become second nature.

Di Indonesia, Anda menginap di mana?

Apa keperluan Anda dan keluarga Anda?

Apakah Anda akan mencari kamar kos di Indonesia?

Test yourself

1 Unscramble the words to make full sentences.

a Dia - AC - lebih - kamar - suka - tanpa.

b hotel - suka - Budi - menginap - lebih - berbintang - di.

c Mereka - singel - suka - kamar - dobel - kamar - daripada - lebih.

2 Insert the word **kurang** into the sentences to negate them.

a Saya suka menginap di penginapan.

b Aku suka menyewa kamar kos.

c Mereka suka menelpon pada akhir minggu.

3 Put the words in English into Indonesian.

a Hari ini (*what date*)?

b Saya menginap di hotel melati (*on January 17*).

c Besok (*September 23*).

4 Put the following questions into English.

a Di mana hotelnya?

b Berapa tarif kamarnya per malam?

c Berapa nomor telepon kantornya?

d Untuk berapa orang tamu?

5 Correct the underlined words.

a <u>Apa</u> alamat Anda?

b Anda bisa memberikan alamatnya <u>ke</u> saya?

c Alamatnya <u>Malam</u> Rusa No. 88.

d <u>Di mana</u> warna rumahnya?

SELF CHECK

	I CAN . . .
○	. . . talk about types of accommodation.
○	. . . express my preferences and make reservations.
○	. . . use the months of the year to talk about dates.
○	. . . ask for and give addresses.
○	. . . ask for, give, and understand Indonesian spelling.

R2 Review 2

1 Match the Indonesian to the English.

a Kamis	**1** *Monday*
b Minggu	**2** *year*
c hari	**3** *Thursday*
d Jum'at	**4** *day*
e Rabu	**5** *Saturday*
f Senin	**6** *Wednesday*
g Sabtu	**7** *week*
h bulan	**8** *Sunday*
i minggu	**9** *Friday*
j tahun	**10** *month*

2 Everyday Indonesian questions are very simple. Give the questions that match the answers.

a Umur aku dua belas tahun.
b Mereka mandi tadi pagi dan tadi sore.
c Aku cari kemeja putih.
d Aku mau beli baterai.
e Ukuranku lima setengah.
f Harganya tiga puluh delapan ribu rupiah.
g Yang panjang.
h Aku menginap di hotel berbintang.
i Alamatnya Jalan Mawar nomor enam.
j Maaf, tidak ada fasilitas internet.

3 Put the following everyday expressions into Indonesian.

a Sleep well.
b Please pay at the till (for your convenience).
c Please wait a moment.
d Do buy (it).
e Today is Tuesday, August 17.
f Sorry.
g The cheapest one.

4 Help Jon complete his Indonesian blog entry by putting the words in English into Indonesian.

Blog Add post

Minggu ini, setiap hari aku (*went to the office*) tanpa (*having breakfast*). Istri adikku berkata, 'Jon, (*this week*) kamu terlalu (*busy*), ya?' Besok pagi, aku (*will wake up*), mandi, dan (*look for*) sepasang sepatu di (*department store*) dan (*souvenirs*) di (*craft and art market*). (*The prices*) tidak mahal. Saya akan lihat (*many*) orang berbelanja (*at the weekend*)!

5 Give the following in English.

- **a** tujuh belas tahun
- **b** seorang insinyur
- **c** sembilan bulan
- **d** sepuluh orang
- **e** tahun seribu tujuh ratus enam puluh dua
- **f** satu juta lima ratus ribu rupiah

6 Anisa has written an email to her penfriend Harjeet to tell him about her family's trip to a shopping mall. Read the email and answer the questions that follow.

New message

Halo Harjeet!

Keluargaku berbelanja di mal kemarin. Bapakku beli radio baru. Warna radio itu cokelat tua. Ibuku beli rok dan jas untuk pergi ke kantor. Ibu juga beli kaos-kaos untuk adik-adikku. Harga kaos yang biru tua seratus lima puluh ribu rupiah. Harga kaos yang biru muda seratus ribu rupiah. Aku beli baterai HP baru dan sepasang sandal kuning. Aku kurang suka warna kuning. Aku lebih suka warna abu-abu tetapi yang abu-abu tidak ada di mal. Apakah ada mal di Wales? Keluarga kamu berbelanja di mana?

Salam,

Anisa

a Who bought the new radio?
b What is the color of the radio?
c Why did Anisa's mother buy a skirt and blazer?
d How much did the light blue T-shirt cost?
e What did Anisa buy?
f Why did she not buy the gray ones?

7 Siti is counting what she can see out of her window. Help her choose the correct classifiers.

a tiga *pasang / ekor* celana	three pairs of pants
b enam *orang / ekor* burung	six birds
c dua *orang / ekor* ilmuwan	two scientists
d empat *pasang / buah* sikat	four brushes

8 Use the contents of the box to complete the sentences so that they match the English translations.

silakan -lah tolong

a cari losmen	*Do look for a guesthouse.*
b bantu saya	*Please help me.*
c menginap di rumah kami	*Please stay at our house.*

9 Match the questions or statements to the replies.

a Maaf.	1 Maaf. Yang ini tidak dijual.
b Terima kasih.	2 Sampai nanti!
c Yang mana lebih murah?	3 Tidak apa-apa.
d Sampai nanti!	4 Artinya '*contactless*'.
e Apa arti 'tanpa sentuh'?	5 Yang ini lebih murah.
f f Aku boleh lihat yang itu?	6 Terima kasih kembali.

10 Unscramble the words to make full sentences.

a pada - malam - Maret - kamar - Berapa - per - tarif - bulan?
b dobel - memesan - Saya - kamar - mau.
c reservasi - Anda - kami - di - ada - hotel - sudah?

11 Bima recently talked to an oral historian about his daily life and his household. Read the historian's transcript and answer the questions that follow.

> Saya karyawan di sebuah perusahaan asing. Istri saya seorang ibu rumah tangga. Dia lebih suka berbelanja di pasar daripada berbelanja di pusat perbelanjaan. Dia bilang kemarin, 'Barang-barang di pasar yang paling murah!' Istri saya berbelanja di pasar setiap hari Jum'at. Rumah kami kecil, tetapi ada pelajar asing tahun ini. Dia orang Australia dan namanya Ian Park. Dia akan pulang pada bulan November.

a Where does Bima work?
b What is his wife's occupation?
c Why does she prefer shopping at the market?
d When does she go to the market?
e Is their house large or small?
f Who is Ian?
g When is Ian returning to Australia?

12 Wati receives a text message from Linda, who is first to arrive at their hotel room. List the room's features.

> Wati, di kamar hotel ada fasilitas internet dan AC. Ada kamar mandi dalam. Ada air panas dan pancuran mandi.

13 Tono receives a text message from Tini not long after he leaves her in a line at the till. Translate her message.

> Tono, di kasir tidak ada kembalian. Saya tidak ada uang pas. Kamu ada uang lima puluh ribu rupiah?

14 **Read the notes about Ningsih and use the information to help her fill in the hotel's registration form.**

Nama dia Ningsih. Nama keluarganya Suparman. Ningsih bekerja di sebuah LSM. Dia lahir pada tanggal dua belas Juli tahun seribu sembilan ratus delapan puluh. Dia tinggal di Jalan Sadikin nomor tiga puluh empat. Rumahnya di kota Jakarta. Kode posnya satu-nol-satu-enam-dua-dua. Nomor telepon dia kosong-dua-satu-lima-tiga-enam-lima-tujuh-kosong-satu.

Hotel Papandayan

a Nama Tamu: ______________________________

b Tanggal Lahir: ______________________________

c Pekerjaan: ______________________________

d Alamat: ______________________________

e Kota: ______________________________

f Kode Pos: ______________________________

g No. Telepon: ______________________________

15 **Linda and Saul Curtis are making enquiries into renting a house in Bali. Read Linda's email to a local property agent and answer the questions that follow.**

New message

Yth. Bapak/Ibu,

Apa kabar? Nama saya Linda Curtis. Saya dan suami saya Saul sudah tinggal di Indonesia selama satu tahun. Tahun ini kami mau menyewa rumah di Bali untuk tiga bulan, dari bulan Juni sampai bulan Agustus. Kami perlu tiga kamar tidur dan dua kamar mandi. Kami kurang suka dapur yang kecil. Kami akan senang kalau ada teras yang besar dan kolam renang juga. Kami bisa bayar uang sewa dalam dolar atau rupiah. Tolong hubungi kami di 0811-2873-62590. Saya tunggu kabar dari Anda.

Salam,

Linda

- **a** How long do they want to rent the house for?
- **b** How many bedrooms and bathrooms do they need?
- **c** What would they not like?
- **d** What extras would they enjoy?
- **e** What did Linda write about the rent money?

7

In this unit, you will learn how to:

» talk about different modes of transport.
» order and buy tickets.
» ask for and give the time.
» talk about the locations *here*, *there*, and *over there*.

Selamat jalan!

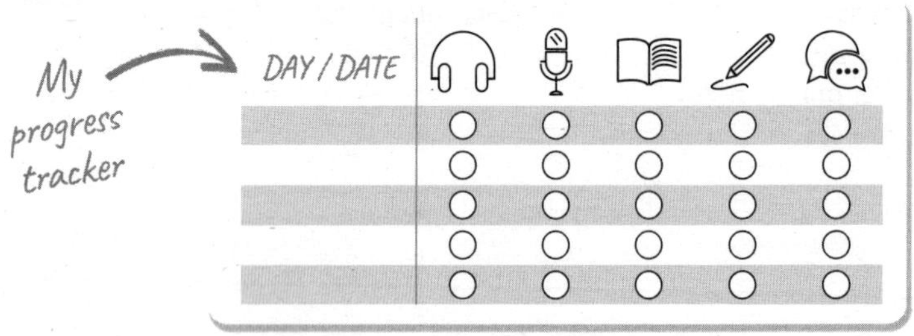

Transportation

Crossing the Indonesian archipelago by **pesawat terbang** or **kapal terbang** (*airplane*) gives you spectacular views of the country's volcanoes. Overland transport such as the intercity **bus** (*bus*) and the **kereta api** (*train*), however, allows you to **naik** (*get on*) or **turun** (*get off*) in smaller towns and cities. Along with the new **kereta bawah tanah** (*underground train*) service, local travel can be done by bus, **taksi** (*taxi*), or the **ojek** (*motorcycle service*) that takes you anywhere you want to go if you are comfortable riding as a **penumpang** (*passenger*) on a motorcycle. Remember to ask how much the **ongkos** (*fare*) is before the **perjalanan** (*journey*) begins. Using **kendaraan umum** (*public transport*) can be convenient, but metered rides are offered only by taxi companies. If you wish to hire a **mobil** (*car*), you may drive it yourself if you have a valid license. In tourist areas, hiring a **sepeda motor** (*motorcycle*) or **sepeda** (*bicycle*) is a great way to get around. To get to Indonesia's smaller islands, cross the waters by **kapal** (*ship*) or **feri** (*ferry*). Transport routes are busiest during **Lebaran**, the holiday marking the end of the fasting month, when many celebrants travel to visit their families.

What do you think the phrase for *trip fare* might be?

Vocabulary builder

07.01 Look at the words and phrases and complete the English translations. Then listen to the recording and imitate the pronunciation of the speakers.

TRAVELING

berangkat	*depart*
sampai	*arrive*
ganti	*switch* (v.), *change* (v.)
kembali	*return* (v.)
loket	*ticket booth*
karcis	*ticket*
jurusan	*destination, heading (for)*
tiket pulang pergi	________ *ticket*
tiket sekali jalan	________ *ticket*
bagasi	*luggage*
koper	*suitcase*
selamat jalan	*have a good journey*
selamat tinggal	*goodbye* (to people you leave behind)

LOCATION

sini	*here*
situ	*there*
sana	*over there*

TIME

jam	*hour*
menit	________
kurang	*less, minus*
lewat	*past*
seperempat	*a quarter*
setengah	*half*

The word **pukul** is also used to mean *hour*. This use is highly formal, usually reserved for the news and telling the time on the radio and television.

NEW EXPRESSIONS

buatkan	*create (for)*
tentu	*of course*
baru	*recently, just, newly*

datang	*come, arrive*
terlambat	*slow, late*

Conversation 1

07.02 *Jon is at the airport, having missed his flight and needing another.*

1 What form of identification does Jon provide?

Soraya	Bisa saya bantu, Pak?
Jon	Masih ada pesawat terbang ke Bali hari ini?
Soraya	Ada, Pak. Ada pesawat yang berangkat pada jam empat kurang seperempat sore.
Jon	Baiklah. Saya mau membeli satu tiket.
Soraya	Bapak mau naik kelas ekonomi atau bisnis?
Jon	Saya mau naik kelas ekonomi.
Soraya	Pulang pergi atau sekali jalan, Pak?
Jon	Pulang pergi.
Soraya	Kapan Bapak mau kembali ke Jakarta?
Jon	Saya belum tahu. Anda bisa buatkan saya tiket tanggal terbuka?
Soraya	Ya. Bisa. Saya boleh lihat paspornya, Pak?
Jon	Tentu boleh. Ini paspor saya.
Soraya	Ada bagasi, Pak?
Jon	Ya, ada satu koper.
Soraya	Ini tiketnya. Selamat jalan, Pak.
Jon	Selamat tinggal.

tiket tanggal terbuka	*open-date ticket*

2 Find the expressions in the conversation that mean:

a travel in economy class ________

b I don't know yet. ________

c Goodbye. ________

3 Read or listen again and answer the questions.

a When is the flight departing?

b What kind of ticket does Jon buy?

c What luggage does Jon have?

4 07.03 Now listen to the lines from the conversation and repeat. Be sure to pay attention to the pronunciation.

Language discovery 1

Look at the sentences from the conversation. Put the words in English into Indonesian.

a Dia mau (*travel in economy class*).

b Pesawat itu berangkat (*at a quarter to four in the afternoon*).

1 TRAVELING

When discussing travel, the word **naik** (*get on*) can be used to mean *traveling in/on, going by, taking, riding*. You can also use **naik** to mean *by*. For example, **kembali ke kantor naik bus** means *return to the office by bus.*

Setiap hari dia naik kendaraan umum ke kantor.

Every day he takes public transport to the office.

Saya pergi naik bus dan dia naik sepeda motornya ke Palu.

I am going by bus and she is riding her motorcycle to Palu.

2 THE TIME

When telling the time, start with the hour. For example**, jam tiga** (*three o'clock*). If it is *five minutes past the hour*, add **lewat lima menit**. If it is *five minutes to the hour*, add **kurang lima menit**. Then, mention the time of day as necessary.

Sekarang jam tiga lewat lima menit sore.

It is now five minutes past three (o'clock) in the afternoon.

You can leave out the word **menit** (*minute*) once you are comfortable without it.

The word **setengah** is also used in telling the time, but it is the reverse of the British usage of *half* so that **setengah dua** (*half two*) means *half past one*.

Saya sampai pada jam setengah dua siang.

I arrive at half past one in the afternoon.

Indonesians also use **seperempat** (*a quarter*) in place of **lima belas menit** (*fifteen minutes*).

Kakek berangkat pada jam tujuh kurang seperempat pagi.

Grandfather left at a quarter to seven in the morning.

To ask about the time, use **jam berapa** (*what hour*).

Jam berapa sekarang? Jam empat.

What time is it now? Four o'clock.

Note that **berapa jam** means *how many hours.*

Practice

1 Put the following sentences into English.

- **a** Jon naik pesawat terbang ke Padang.
- **b** Ita naik sepeda motor ke rumah ibunya.
- **c** Dimas naik kereta bawah tanah ke kantor.

2 Put the following times into Indonesian.

- **a** 11:15 a.m.
- **b** 08:50 a.m.
- **c** 06:30 p.m.

3 07.04 Now use the times to prepare responses to the questions below. Then, listen and answer in real time. Do this as many times as you need to for it to become second nature.

Jam berapa kereta api berangkat?

Pada jam berapa ferinya akan sampai di Lombok?

Untuk jam berapa Anda mau memesan taksi?

Pronunciation

There are two pronunciations of the letter **e** in Indonesian. They can both be found in the word **sepeda** (*bicycle*). In older reading material, the second **e** may be spelled as **é** to differentiate the sounds. Currently, the only way to familiarize yourself with the different pronunciations is to hear the words being spoken.

07.05 Listen to the two pronunciations of the letter *e* and repeat.

1 sepeda
2 mereka
3 sewa
4 seperempat
5 kereta

Speaking

1 **07.06 Look at Helen's schedule and talk about it in Indonesian using the 12-hour clock.**

07:00	go to the office by car
12:00	go to lunch by bus
13:30	return to the office by motorcycle service
17:20	return home by car

2 **Now talk about your own schedule in Indonesian.**

Conversation 2

07.07 *Linda has just got off the bus at a station. She now needs to get on a different bus to get to Solo.*

1 How much time is left before the bus departs?

Linda	Permisi, Pak. Saya harus ganti bus. Di mana saya bisa naik bus jurusan Solo?
Abdul	Bus itu baru berangkat. Mau ke mana, Bu?
Linda	Mau ke Solo.
Abdul	Bus berikutnya bus jurusan Semarang. Bus itu berhenti di Solo. Naik bus itu dan turun di Solo.
Linda	Di mana saya bisa naik bus jurusan Semarang?
Abdul	Ibu bisa naik bus jurusan Semarang di sini.
Linda	Jam berapa busnya berangkat?
Abdul	Busnya berangkat pada jam satu lewat seperempat siang.
Linda	Jam berapa sekarang?
Abdul	Jam satu kurang sepuluh.
Linda	Oh, masih ada dua puluh lima menit.
Abdul	Ya, Ibu ada waktu. Ibu tidak akan terlambat.
Linda	Di mana saya bisa membeli karcis bus?
Abdul	Di dalam bus atau di loket, tetapi lebih baik di loket. Loketnya di situ.

berhenti	*stop* (v.)
berikut	*following, next*
waktu	*time*

2 Match the Indonesian to the English.

- **a** Mau ke Solo.
- **b** Jam berapa sekarang?
- **c** Jam berapa busnya berangkat?

- **1** *What time is it now?*
- **2** *What time is the bus leaving?*
- **3** *I'm going to Solo.*

3 Check, then cover up your answers and see if you can say them without looking at the conversation.

4 Read or listen again and answer the following questions.

- **a** What bus does Linda need to get?
- **b** When is the next bus departing?
- **c** Where can Linda buy a bus ticket?

5 07.08 Now listen to the lines from the conversation and repeat. Then listen to Linda's lines and respond as Abdul.

Language discovery 2

Look at the sentences from the conversation. Find the sentences in Indonesian that mean the following.

a The ticket booth is there.

b That bus just departed.

c Where are you going, Madam?

1 *HERE, THERE,* AND *OVER THERE*

When you use the location words **sini** (*here*), **situ** (*there*), and **sana** (*over there*), they should always be combined with either the preposition **di** (*at/in/on*), **ke** (*to*), or **dari** (*from*).

naik bus di sini	*get on the bus here*
loket di situ	*the ticket booth is there*
terbang ke sana dari sini	*fly over there from here*

2 IF SOMETHING JUST HAPPENED

The word **baru** (*new*) can be used to talk about how something only recently or just happened. For example, you can say that **dia baru datang** to mean *he recently came* or *he just came*.

3 WHEN 'WANT (TO GO)' MEANS 'GOING'

The phrase **mau pergi** (*want to go*) can also mean *intend to go* or *are going* if it is used when you're already on your way. Whilst you're traveling, you may be asked, **Kamu mau pergi ke mana?** to mean *Where are you going?* Since this question is often asked in everyday situations when people are in a hurry, the pronoun **Anda** or **kamu** (*you*) and the word **pergi** (*go*) is often omitted so that the question becomes **Mau ke mana?** (*Going where?*) You can reply, **Mau ke Solo**, for example, to mean *I'm going to Solo.*

Practice

1 **Put the following sentences into Indonesian.**
   - **a** Your bus will stop there.
   - **b** You can buy your bus ticket here.
   - **c** Jon departed from (over) there at half past four in the afternoon.

2 **Put the following sentences into English.**
   - **a** Pesawat terbang dari Ambon baru sampai.
   - **b** Dia baru beli tiket pesawat.
   - **c** Mereka baru bayar ongkos perjalanan.

3 **07.09 Practice asking and answering questions about where you want to go or are going to go.**

Listening

1 **07.10 Listen to the dialogue and answer the following questions.**

Berapa lama	*How long, What is the duration of*
kira-kira	*roughly, at a guess*
jalan kaki	*walk, travel on foot*
sewaktu	*while, when*

   - **a** What times are the trains?
   - **b** How long is the journey?
   - **c** How much is the ticket that she buys?

2 **07.11 Listen to the dialogue and match the travel plan to the suggested transport option.**

a traveling to Trawas	*1 by taxi*
b going to Madura	*2 by motorcycle service*
c going into the city	*3 go on foot*
d getting to the market	*4 by ship*
e when you have no time	*5 by car*

3 07.12 Read the questions below and prepare responses that are true for you. Then, listen and respond in real time.

Jam berapa sekarang?

Pada jam berapa Anda berangkat dari rumah?

Pada jam berapa Anda sampai di kantor?

Reading and writing

1 Read the letter Samuel Lim has written to his Indonesian-speaking grandmother about his travels in Indonesia so far.

> *Yth. Nenek,*
>
> *Aku datang ke Indonesia pada bulan Maret. Pada bulan April, aku naik kereta api dari Jakarta ke Yogyakarta. Tiketnya tidak mahal. Perjalanan dari sini ke sana sembilan jam. Kalau naik pesawat dari Jakarta ke Yogyakarta hanya kira-kira satu jam. Sewaktu di Yogyakarta aku suka naik ojek dan jalan kaki. Banyak orang naik sepeda. Aku kembali ke Jakarta naik bus. Di Jakarta, aku naik kereta bawah tanah setiap hari.*
>
> *Samuel*

2 Imagine you're traveling in Indonesia. Write a letter about your travels and how you're getting around.

Go further

In Indonesia, there are three recognized time zones, which you might come across in the news or while traveling eastwards or westwards from one end of the country to the other.

Waktu Indonesia Barat (WIB)	Western Indonesia Time
Waktu Indonesia Tengah (WITA)	Central Indonesia Time
Waktu Indonesia Timur (WIT)	Eastern Indonesia Time

On the news broadcast from the capital Jakarta, for example, you would hear the time announced as **pukul sembilan malam WIB** (*nine o'clock in the evening Western Indonesia Time*).

If you want to talk about getting around at certain times of day instead of at a specific hour, you can combine the concepts you have learned so far.

1 Complete the English translations.

a pada pagi hari — *In the _______*

b pada siang hari — *In the day (between _______ a.m. and _______ p.m.)*

c pada sore hari — *In the _______*

d pada malam hari — *In the _______ or at night*

2 Put the following sentences into Indonesian.

a I arrived in Indonesia at night.

b I departed in the morning.

c I will take the underground train in the early afternoon.

d She will come to Lembang by train in the late afternoon.

As you have seen, the word **datang** can mean both *come* and *arrive*. When there is a difference, it lies in the preposition you use so that **datang di** means *arrive at* and **datang ke** means *come to*. The combination **datang dari** can mean both *arrive from* and *come from*, whether the place refers to your last place of embarkation or where your journey began.

3 07.13 Read the questions below and prepare your own responses. Then, listen and respond. Do this as many times as you need to for it to become second nature.

a Pukul berapa sekarang di kota Anda?

b Anda datang dari mana?

c Kamu mau datang ke rumahku?

d Selamat datang di Indonesia! Kapan kamu sampai?

Test yourself

1 Put the words in English into Indonesian.

Amir naik (*airplane*) dari Jakarta ke Medan dengan (*one-way ticket*). (*Journey*) dia kira-kira dua jam. Di Medan Amir (*went by car*) ke rumah keluarganya. Amir dan Samsul, adik laki-laki Amir, (*traveled by taxi*) ke bank mereka. Malam itu, Amir (*used a motorcycle service*) ke Belawan. Dari Belawan, dia (*got on*) kapal (*heading for*) Kepulauan Riau dan (*got off*) di pulau Batam.

2 Put the following phrases into English.

a jam empat kurang dua puluh sore
b jam sembilan lewat seperempat pagi
c jam setengah delapan malam
d jam dua belas siang

3 Unscramble the words to make full sentences.

a jurusan-datang? - Pada - Madiun - berapa - jam - bus
b malam. - mereka - sebelas - pada - Mobil - jam - sampai
c mau - Jam - berangkat? - Anda-berapa
d berapa - berangkat? - kereta - Jam - berikutnya

4 Choose the correct word to match the phrases with the English translations.

a datang ke *sini / sana* — *come here*
b sampai di *sini / sana* — *arrive over there*
c berangkat dari *sini / situ* — *depart from there*

5 Put the following sentences into Indonesian.

a The ship just departed.
b The passengers just got off the ferry.

6 Choose the question that doesn't mean *Where are you going?*

a Mau ke mana?
b Mau di mana?
c Anda mau pergi ke mana?

SELF CHECK

	I CAN . . .
●	. . . talk about different modes of transport.
●	. . . order and buy tickets.
●	. . . ask for and give the time.
●	. . . talk about the locations *here*, *there*, and *over there*.

8

In this unit, you will learn how to:

» talk about food.
» read and order items from a menu.
» ask for and understand suggestions.
» ask for the check.
» talk about doing things together.

Mari memesan! Kamu mau makan apa?

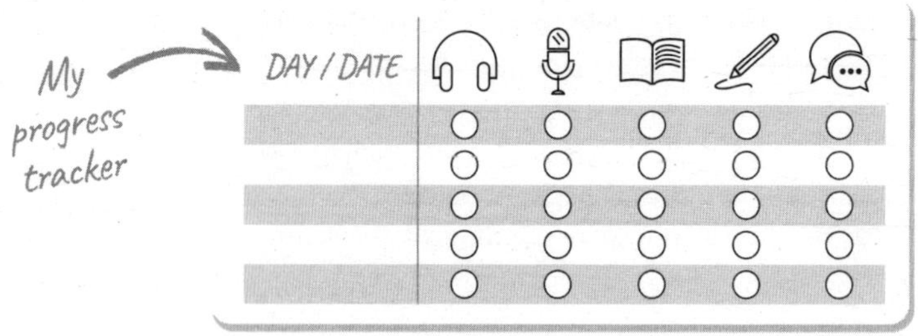

Cuisine

Most Indonesians prefer savoury breakfast dishes, but eating **roti** (*bread*) is now more common and **roti bakar** (*toast, grilled sandwich*) is served in hotels and as **enak** (*delicious*) street food. Lunch may come in the form of **sepiring nasi goreng** (*a plate of fried rice*) or **semangkok mie telur rebus** (*a bowl of egg noodle soup*), single-dish meals served to those on the go. In the afternoon, you may be interested in tasting **secangkir kopi jahe** (*a cup of ginger coffee*) with some **bolu kukus** (*steamed sponge cake*) or enjoying **segelas jus alpukat** (*a glass of avocado juice*), often mixed with chocolate and served cold. When dining together, Indonesians enjoy sharing dishes served all at the same time instead of in succession. A luxurious but harmonious meal would contain a combination of **ikan** (*fish*), meat such as **daging ayam** (*chicken*), shellfish such as **udang** (*shrimp*), **sayur-sayur** (*vegetables*), **tahu** (*tofu*), and **tempe** (*fermented soy bean cake*) cooked in a variety of ways. Many Indonesian dishes are prepared using **santan** (*coconut milk*) or soy sauce, but each regional **masakan** (*cuisine*) is typified by a particular flavor or ingredient. Javanese cooking, for example, is **manis** (*sweet*), Madurese food is **asin** (*salty*), and Padang cuisine is **pedas** (*spicy*).

If **dua porsi nasi** means *two portions of rice*, how would you say *a portion of rice*?

Vocabulary builder

1 08.01 **Look at the words and phrases. First, match the Indonesian to the English. Next, use the words in the box to complete the English translations. Then, listen to the recording and imitate the pronunciation of the speakers.**

> While some Indonesian dishes have individual names, many are also listed in menus according to how they are prepared.

COOKING METHODS

a goreng	**1** *to boil, boiled*
b rebus	**2** *to roast/grill, roasted/grilled*
c bakar/panggang	**3** *to stir-fry, stir-fried*
d kukus	**4** *to fry, fried*
e tumis	**5** *to steam, steamed*

POPULAR MENU ITEMS

> soup, prawn cracker, curry, meat skewer

krupuk udang ________
sate ________
kare ________
sop ________

OTHER STAPLE FOODS

singkong	*cassava*	**sagu**	*sago*
bubur	*porridge*	**lontong**	*steamed rice cake*

NEW EXPRESSIONS

kalian	*you, your* (plural, informal)
ingin	*want, wish*
pesan	*order* (v.)
minum	*drink* (v.)
minta	*request, ask for*
semua	*all*
yang	*the one that is, the ones that are, the ... one/ones*
ambilkan	*to fetch*
selesai	*to be finished, to be done*
bon	*check, bill*
angkat	*to lift (up), clear* (coll., v.)
bersama	*together, (along) with*
bagaimana kalau	*how would it be if,* (coll.) *what about*

DRINKS

air	*water*
kopi	*coffee*
teh	*tea*
es teh	*iced tea*
air jeruk	*citrus drink*
jus jeruk	*citrus (orange, clementine) juice*
susu kedelai	*soy milk*
bir	*beer*

> To avoid drinking unsanitary water, ask for **air mineral** (*mineral water*) or **air botol** (*bottled water*).

USEFUL WORDS

panas	*hot*	**dingin**	*cold*
hangat	*warm*	**tawar**	*plain*
pahit	*bitter*	**asam**	*sour*
garam	*salt*	**merica**	*pepper*

If the high level of sweetness in Indonesian drinks does not suit your tastes, you can order your drink **tawar** (*plain*), for example as **teh tawar** (*unsweetened tea*), before adding your preferred amount of **gula** (*sugar*). The exception is unsweetened coffee, which must be ordered as **kopi pahit** (*bitter coffee*) or **kopi hitam** (*black coffee*).

sapi	*cow*
kambing	*goat*
babi	*pig*
kepiting	*crab*
jeruk	*citrus (clementine, lime, orange)*
pisang	*banana, plantain*
kelapa	*coconut*
kacang	*nut, pea, bean*
jagung	*corn*
kentang	*potato*

When talking about food, the words for land animals must be prefaced with the word for *meat*. For example, **babi** is *pig* but **daging babi** is *pork*. Many people do not eat pork in Indonesia. Due to the widespread availability of soy protein products, it is also rather easy to have a completely meat-free diet. Do you remember how to say *I do not eat …?*

2 08.02 Listen to the drinks, useful words, and shopping list and imitate the pronunciation of the speakers.

Conversation 1

08.03 *A family of three arrives at a restaurant.*

1 What drinks do they order?

Pelayan	Selamat datang di Restoran Ibu Munir.
Ibu	Selamat siang. Ada meja untuk empat orang?
Pelayan	Ada. Silakan duduk. Ini menunya.
Ibu	Anak-anak, kalian ingin makan apa?
Tono	Saya ingin makan kare ikan dan tempe goreng. Saya ingin minum es teh manis.
Tini	Pak, apakah saya boleh meminta secangkir teh panas dan sepiring mie goreng sayur?
Pelayan	Tentu boleh. Ibu mau memesan apa?
Ibu	Saya ingin mencoba mienya. Yang mana enak?
Pelayan	Semua mie kami enak.
Ibu	Saya suka yang pedas. Yang mana pedas?
Pelayan	Mie telur kami pedas. Ibu ingin coba mie telur?
Ibu	Baiklah. Saya ingin pesan semangkok mie telur rebus, segelas es kopi, dan dua porsi sate ayam.
Tono	Kami juga mau sop bayam, air dingin tanpa es, dan nasi untuk dua orang.

[*The server leaves and returns with their order.*]

Pelayan	Ini pesanan Anda. Ini minuman-minuman Anda. Dan ini makanan Anda datang sekarang.
Tono	Pak, tolong ambilkan saya satu sedotan.
Pelayan	Maaf. Ini sedotannya. Selamat makan.

duduk	*sit*
meja	*table*
bayam	*spinach*
sedotan	*straw*

2 Find the expressions in the conversation that mean:

a Which one is the delicious one? ________

b And here is your food coming now. ________

c Please fetch me a straw. ________

3 Read or listen again and answer the questions.

a What has the mother ordered?

b What was Tono missing?

c What do you think *Selamat makan* means?

4 08.04 **Now listen to the lines from the conversation and repeat. Be sure to pay attention to the pronunciation.**

Language discovery 1

Look at the sentences from the conversation. Put the words in English into Indonesian.

a Ibu mau (*order*) apa?

b Ini (*order*) Anda.

c Saya ingin memesan (*a cup*) teh panas.

d Saya suka (*the spicy ones*). Yang mana (*spicy*)?

1 MORE ABOUT VERBS

One important verbal prefix is **meX-**, the **X** standing for a letter that changes depending on the first letter of the verb's root word. For example, the word **pesan** becomes **memesan** (*order*).

If the root word begins with a vowel, **meX-** becomes **meng-** so that **ajar** becomes **mengajar** (*teach*).

If the root word begins with b, f, or p, **meX-** becomes **mem-** so that **beli** becomes **membeli** (*buy*) and, because you have to drop the p, **pakai** becomes **memakai** (*wear, use*).

If the root word begins with c, d, j, t, sy, or z, **meX-** becomes **men-** so that **cari** becomes **mencari** (*look for*), **jual** becomes **menjual** (*sell*). You would also drop the t so that, for example, **tunggu** becomes **menunggu** (*wait*).

If the root word for the verb begins with g, h, k, or kh, **meX-** becomes **meng-** so that **ganti** becomes **mengganti** (*change*).

If the root word begins with s, **meX-** becomes **meny-** so that the word **sewa** becomes **menyewa** (*rent*).

If the root word begins with l, m, n, ny, ng, r, w, or y, there is no change and **meX-** becomes **me-** so that **masak**, for example, becomes **memasak** (*cook*).

Whenever you come across an unfamiliar verb that begins with **meX-**, knowing how **X** changes helps you look up the verb's meaning because in a dictionary, a verb is always listed under its root word.

Indonesian speakers sometimes drop the **me-** while keeping the related **X** sound change. For example, when **goreng** is transformed into **menggoreng** (*fry*), what you might hear in everyday speech is **nggoreng**.

2 TURNING VERBS INTO NOUNS USING THE SUFFIX –AN

A basic Indonesian noun can be created out of a basic verb by adding the suffix **-an** to the end of the original word. Adding **-an** to **pesan** (*to order*) will give you **pesanan** (*an order, what you order*), for example. Adding **-an** to **masak** (*cook*) will give you **masakan** (*cooking* or *cuisine, what you cook* or *dish*).

3 USING THE SE– PREFIX WHEN ORDERING

As you have previously seen, the **se-** prefix is used in counting to mean *one* of something. When ordering food or drink, attach the **se-** prefix to the tableware or container used for serving.

Saya mau semangkok (*or* satu mangkok) bubur ayam.

I want one bowl of chicken porridge.

Saya mau sebotol (*or* satu botol) bir.

I want one bottle of beer.

When you order an item without specifying how you want it served, you should use **satu** (*one*) instead of the **se-** prefix.

Saya mau memesan satu es teh tawar.

I want to order one unsweetened (or *plain*) *iced tea.*

4 SUGGESTIONS

While you can ask for a suggestion by asking **Apa saran Anda?** (*What is your suggestion?*), Indonesians are more likely to first state their preferences before asking for suitable menu items to be pointed out to them. For example, you first state that you like **yang asin** (*the salty ones* or *the ones that are salty*) to mean you like **makanan yang asin** (*food that is salty*). Then, you would ask **Yang mana asin?** (*Which ones are salty?*)

Saya suka yang tidak pedas. Yang mana tidak pedas?

I like the ones that are not spicy. Which ones are not spicy?

Saya mau minuman yang manis. Yang mana manis?

I want a drink that is sweet. Which ones are sweet?

Food or drink suggestions are usually made by asking people to **coba** (*try*) something or whether they wish to try something.

Kalau Anda suka yang manis, cobalah jus jeruk.

If you like the ones that are sweet, try the orange juice.

Anda ingin coba krupuk udang?

Do you wish to try the prawn crackers?

Practice

1 Give the Indonesian root words for the following verbs, then complete the English translation of the verbs.

- **a** merebus ________ ________
- **b** menggoreng ________ ________
- **c** mengukus ________ ________

2 Turn the verbs into nouns and complete the English translation of the nouns.

- **a** makan ________ ________
- **b** minum ________ ________
- **c** masak ________ ________

3 Put the following sentences into English.

- **a** Kakek ingin memesan secangkir kopi hitam.
- **b** Adik perempuanku tidak mau semangkok sup ayam.
- **c** Mereka ingin seporsi ikan bakar kecap.

4 08.05 Practice telling others what you like and then asking for suitable suggestions.

Saya suka yang tidak pahit. Yang mana tidak pahit?

Pronunciation

08.06 Several Indonesian words have two or more accepted pronunciations either because they can be spelled in different ways or due to regional differences. Listen to how the following words are pronounced and repeat.

1 telur	telor
2 santan	santen
3 asam	asem
4 sop	sup
5 saos	saus

Speaking

08.07 Read the questions below and prepare your own responses. Then, listen and respond in real time. Do this as many times as you need to for it to become second nature.

Anda ingin memesan apa?

Anda mau meja untuk berapa orang?

Conversation 2

08.08 *Ani and Affandi are at the end of their meal.*

1 What does Affandi think is very delicious?

Ani	Makanan di rumah makan ini enak, ya? Kamu mau satu porsi ikan panggang lagi?
Affandi	Rasanya enak sekali tetapi aku sudah kenyang. Kamu masih lapar?
Ani	Tidak. Kita sudah selesai, ya?
Affandi	Ya. Sudah. Aku akan minta bonnya. Permisi, Pak. Kami boleh minta bonnya?
Ani	Dia tidak dengar kamu. Coba minta sekali lagi.

Affandi	Permisi, Pak. Tolong ambilkan bonnya.
Pelayan	Ya, Pak. Saya ambilkan. Sudah selesai makan, ya? Kami boleh angkat semua dari meja?
Affandi	Ya. Silakan. Terima kasih. Ani, kamu mau makan bersama lagi pada hari Jum'at?
Ani	Maaf. Jum'at ini saya akan makan bersama Yati.
Affandi	Kalau begitu, bagaimana kalau hari Sabtu?
Ani	Sabtu? Bisa. Aku bisa makan bersama kamu pada hari Sabtu.

rasa	*flavor, taste, feel*
lapar	*hungry*
kenyang	*full*
dengar	*hear*

2 Find the expressions in the conversation that mean:

a very delicious ________
b still hungry ________
c have finished ________
d eat together ________

3 Check, then cover up your answers and see if you can say them without looking at the conversation.

4 Read or listen again and answer the following questions.

a What do you think *rumah makan* means?
b Why does Affandi have to flag the server twice?
c What does the server ask for permission to do?
d When are they planning to eat together again?

5 08.09 Now listen to the lines from the conversation and repeat. Then listen to Affandi's lines and respond as Ani.

Language discovery 2

Look at the sentences from the conversation. Put the words in English into Indonesian..

a Kamu mau (*another plate of curry*)?
b Tolong (*fetch the check*).
c Kamu mau makan (*together*) pada akhir minggu?

1 ORDERING MORE

You can use the word **lagi** (*again, more*) to order more food or drink by placing it after the thing or things you want more of.

Satu gelas air jeruk hangat lagi, ya?

Another (or *one more*) *glass of the warm citrus drink, please.*

2 ASKING FOR THE CHECK/BILL

Traditionally, the check or bill is calculated by the cashier and not the servers. Hence, you could ask the server to fetch the check or make a request for the check. Where a check is not available, for instance at a street stall, you can ask **Berapa semua?** (*How much is it all?*)

Tolong ambilkan bonnya.	*Please fetch the check.*
Boleh saya minta bonnya?	*May I ask for the check?*

3 DOING THINGS TOGETHER

The word **bersama** (*together*) can be used after verbs when you want to say that you are doing an activity with others.

Tjin dan Sri makan bersama. Saya makan bersama Santi.

Tjin and Sri eat together. I eat (along) with Santi.

Anda mau makan siang bersama kami?

Do you want to eat lunch with us?

You can also invite others to do an activity with you or signal the start of a shared activity using the word **Mari** (*Let's, Come*).

Mari makan. *Let's eat. Come eat.*

Practice

1 **Put the following sentences into English.**
   a Ayah mau sepiring nasi ayam lagi.
   b Tiga porsi sate kambing lagi, ya?

2 **Put the following sentences into Indonesian.**
   a Please fetch our check.
   b Please ask for the check.

3 **08.10 Practice inviting others to eat with you.**

Listening

dibawa pulang	*carried/taken away* (lit. *taken home*)
dibungkus	*wrapped (to go)*
sehat	*healthy*
haus	*thirsty*

1 08.11 **Linda is at a food stall, ordering lunch. Listen to the dialogue and answer the following questions.**

a Is the food to be eaten there or to be taken away?

b What does the vendor say is healthy and delicious?

c What does Linda take to go?

Vendors who sell drinks in glass bottles will need those bottles back. Ask for your drink to be **dibungkus** (*wrapped*) and they will pour it into a container for you.

2 08.12 **Read the menu and prepare a takeaway order that you'd like to eat. Then, listen and respond in real time.**

Mau pesan apa?

Menu Warung Pak Bejo

sate sapi	*pisang goreng*
udang bakar	*tumis bayam*
ayam lada hitam	*kentang goreng*
sate Padang	*nasi*
sop tahu	*mie*
kepiting asam manis	*lontong*

Reading and writing

1 Shinta and Amir have left a meal on the dining table for their children to eat. Read their note to the children.

Anak-anak, Ibu dan Ayah akan makan malam di rumah kolega kami malam ini. Kalian harus makan bersama, ya? Di meja makan ada makanan yang sehat untuk kalian semua. Ada nasi, ayam panggang, tumis kacang panjang, dan singkong rebus. Ada juga bolu kukus coklat dari Nenek. Selamat makan!

2 You have prepared some delicious Indonesian dishes and drinks for your friends but unfortunately you can't be there to enjoy the lunch with them. Complete the note.

Teman-teman, maaf, ya? Saya tidak bisa ...

Go further

The basic Indonesian cutlery combination is the **garpu** (*fork*) and the **sendok** (*spoon*), but eating with one's hands is a valued tradition. It would be polite to wash or clean your hands before eating and to use your right hand to convey food to your mouth.

1 Match the Indonesian to the English.

a sumpit	*knife*
b sendok teh	*kitchen knife*
c pisau	*chopsticks*
d pisau dapur	*cutlery*
e sendok garpu	*teaspoon*

CONDIMENTS

2 Use the words in the box to complete the English translations.

sweet soy sauce chili sauce soy sauce

a kecap asin ________
b kecap manis ________
c saos sambal ________

The word for peanut is **kacang tanah**, but **saos kacang** or **bumbu kacang** is usually taken to mean *peanut sauce*.

If you have food allergies, you can easily tell others that you **tidak boleh** (*are not allowed*) eat or drink something. You can also explain that you have an allergy using the prefix **ber-** (*to have*) or the word **punya** (*to have*) with the word **alergi** (*allergy*).
Saya tidak boleh makan dan minum yang manis.
I am not allowed to eat and drink sweet things.
Saya beralergi (*or* **punya alergi) kacang tanah.**
I have an allergy to peanuts.

3 08.13 **Read the questions below and prepare your own responses. Then, listen and respond. Check the glossary if there are words you don't know.**

a Anda perlu sendok garpu?
b Anda boleh minum minuman beralkohol?
c Anda punya alergi?

Test yourself

1 Put the following sentences into English.

a Kami akan menunggu makanan kami.
b Pak Bejo membungkus minuman mereka.
c Dia membawa pulang masakan Yati.
d Saya ingin mengganti pesanan saya.

2 Insert the **-an** suffix into the sentences to correct them.

a Bubur sagu makan dari Maluku.
b Babi panggang masak tradisional di Toba.
c Air jeruk hangat minum sehat.

3 Put the following sentences into Indonesian.

a I wish to order a glass of cold water and two glasses of beer.
b His wife wants to eat a portion of steamed rice cake.
c My children want one grilled fish and two beef fried noodles.
d They want four cups of unsweetened tea.

4 Unscramble the words to make full sentences.

a tidak - mana - Yang - asin?
b manis, - Anda - goreng. - suka - singkong - yang - cobalah - Kalau
c coba - kedelai - ingin - kami? - susu - Mereka
d tidak - daging. - makan - Saya

5 Use the words in the box to recreate the phrases below.

satu lagi nasi kopi dua lagi porsi

a another coffee
b two more portions of rice

6 Match the Indonesian to the English.

a Berapa semua?	**1** *Please fetch the check.*
b Tolong ambilkan bonnya.	**2** *May I ask for the check?*
c Saya boleh minta bonnya?	**3** *How much is it all?*

7 Put the words in English into Indonesian.

a Mereka mau memasak (*together*).
b Bernard mau makan (*with*) saya?
c (*Let's*) makan sekarang.
d (*Who*) mau (*order together*)?

SELF CHECK

	I CAN . . .
○	. . . talk about food.
○	. . . read and order items from a menu.
○	. . . ask for and understand suggestions.
○	. . . ask for the check.
○	. . . talk about doing things together.

9

In this unit, you will learn how to:
» ask for and understand directions.
» understand sequences using words and numbers.
» accept or refuse an offer of help.
» recognize warnings.
» ask and explain how to do something.

Bagaimana cara jalan kaki ke bioskop?

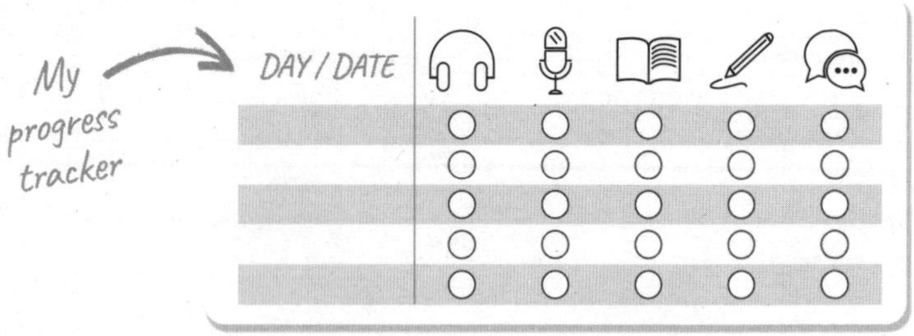

Finding your way

One of the **tempat-tempat** (*places*) worth visiting when you go to a historic city in Indonesia is the **alun-alun** (*square*), where people gather for events or simply pass the time. Take public transport if it is **jauh** (*far*) from where you are and try walking if it is **dekat** (*near*). If you are worried about losing your way, know that Indonesians are always happy to assist people who are **tersesat** (*lost*) or in need of **bantuan** (*help*). Some may even offer to **antar** (*escort*) you to your destination or ask you to **ikut** (*follow*) them there. Their generosity can be a great help because every culture has its own **cara** (*method*) of navigating and it may take practice to make sense of the directions you get. Asking about what you'll find along the way is also helpful, not to mention a fantastic way of making your own local **peta** (*map*). First-time visitors to the country may find the lack of a **trotoar** (*pavement*) along many streets disconcerting at first so do go **hati-hati** (*carefully*) when **berjalan-jalan** (*walking about*) and **menyeberang** (*crossing*) roads. Go **pelan-pelan** (*slowly*) instead of **cepat-cepat** (*quickly*) and enjoy what the city has to offer.

How would you say *I need help* in Indonesian?

Vocabulary builder

09.01 Look at the words and phrases and match the Indonesian places to the English. Then listen to the recording and imitate the pronunciation of the speakers.

PLACES

a	**kantor pos**	1	*crossing, crosswalk*
b	**kantor polisi**	2	*cinema*
c	**stasiun kereta**	3	*embassy*
d	**halte bus**	4	*public restroom*
e	**bandara, bandar udara**	5	*post office*
f	**kedutaan**	6	*police station*
g	**warnet**	7	*train station*
h	**bioskop**	8	*parking space, car park*
i	**tempat parkir**	9	*airport*
j	**tempat penyeberangan**	10	*bus stop*
k	**WC umum**	11	*internet café* (lit. *internet stall*)

A popular euphemism for the *restroom* is **kamar kecil**.

LOCATIONS

belakang	*back*	**depan**	*front*
sebelah	*side*	**samping**	*side*
antara	*between*	**seberang**	*other side*
atas	*above*	**bawah**	*below*
luar	*outside*	**dalam**	*inside*

NEW EXPRESSIONS

numpang tanya ...	*may I ask ...*
bagaimana cara	*what is the method, how does one*
begini	*like this*
pertama	*first, firstly*
belok	*to turn*
lalu, kemudian	*then*
lampu merah	*red light,* (coll.) *traffic light*
terus	(*continue*) *onwards*
lurus	*straight*
persimpangan	*intersection*
terakhir	*last, finally*
repot	*busy, overburdened*

Conversation 1

09.02 *Ian asks Wibowo for some directions.*

1 Where does Ian want to go?

Ian Numpang tanya, di mana kedutaan Inggris?

Wibowo Kedutaan Inggris di alun-alun, di antara kantor polisi dan kantor pos.

Ian Saya tidak ada peta. Alun-alun jauh dari sini?

Wibowo Oh, tidak. Tidak jauh. Alun-alun dekat. Anda bisa jalan kaki ke sana.

Ian Bagaimana cara jalan kaki ke sana?

Wibowo Caranya begini, Anda harus ambil Jalan Adipati. Pertama, keluar hotel dan belok kanan. Lalu, jalan kaki terus sampai lampu merah kedua. Belok kiri di persimpangan itu dan terus lurus sampai Anda masuk alun-alun. Anda akan lihat kedutaannya di seberang alun-alun.

Ian Jadi terakhir saya harus menyeberang alun-alun?

Wibowo Ya, betul.

Ian Di lampu merah kedua ada apa?

Wibowo Ada apa ya? Oh, ada gereja Katolik. Kalau tidak salah, nama gerejanya Santa Maria.

kanan	*right*
kiri	*left*
keluar	*exit* (v.)
masuk	*enter*

2 **Match the Indonesian word to its opposite, then complete the English translations.**

a dekat	**1** kanan	_____
b pertama	**2** jauh	_____
c kiri	**3** salah	_____
d betul	**4** terakhir	_____

3 **Read or listen again and answer the questions.**

a What does Ian not have?

b What places are to the left and right of where Ian wants to go?

c What street should Ian take to get to the square?

d What is at the second traffic light?

4 **09.03 Now listen to the lines from the conversation and repeat. Be sure to pay attention to the pronunciation.**

Language discovery 1

Look at the sentences from the conversation. Put the words in English into Indonesian.

a (*How do I*) jalan kaki ke sana?

b Jalan kaki terus sampai lampu merah (*second*).

c Anda akan lihat kedutaannya (*across*) alun-alun.

1 GETTING DIRECTIONS

Instead of asking for the **arah jalan** (*street direction*), many Indonesians will ask for **cara naik mobil** (*the way to go by car*) or **cara jalan kaki** (*the way to walk*) to where they are going. Sometimes people omit the mode of travel if it is obvious. The question word **bagaimana** (*how*) is used as you're asking for a method instead of a direction, so that **bagaimana cara** means *how does one* or, loosely, *how do I* do something.

Bagaimana cara naik mobil ke Blok M?

How does one go by car to Blok M?

Bagaimana cara ke kantor polisi dari sini?

How does one (travel) to the police station from here?

2 ORDINAL NUMBERS

Using the **ke-** prefix transforms cardinal numbers into ordinal numbers such as **kedua** (*second*), **ketiga** (*third*), etc. The exception is **pertama** (*first*).

3 TALKING ABOUT LOCATIONS

When you describe where one thing is in relation to another, you should use **di** (*at/in/on*) before the second location. In some cases, for example with a location such as **seberang** (*other side*), it allows you to say **di seberang** (*across*). In other cases, **di** (*at/in/on*) is simply necessary.

Halte bus di seberang jalan dari apotek.

The bus stop is across the street from the pharmacy.

Mobil saya di belakang kantor.

My car is behind the office. (lit.) *My car is at the back of the office.*

Kamar kecil di dalam. Saya tunggu Anda di luar.

The toilet is inside. I will wait for you outside.

When using **kiri** (*left*) or **kanan** (*right*), you'd say, for example, **di sebelah kiri** or **di samping kiri** to mean *on the left side of*.

Practice

1 Put the following questions into Indonesian.

- **a** How does one go to the train station?
- **b** How does one get to the car park?
- **c** How does one walk to the bank from here?

2 Match the Indonesian to the English.

a pertama	**1** *fourth*
b keenam	**2** *first*
c keempat	**3** *sixth*

3 09.04 Describe the places on your local main street or in your neighborhood in relation to one another.

Pronunciation

09.05 Indonesians sometimes omit or drop an e **sound that comes after a consonant and before a syllable that begins with the letter** *r*. **Listen to how the following words are pronounced, first with the** e **included and then with the** e **omitted, and repeat.**

1 seberang

2 menyeberang

3 perahu

4 terima kasih

Speaking

09.06 Read the questions below and prepare responses that are true for you. Then, listen and respond in real time.

Di mana halte bus yang paling dekat?

Bagaimana cara pergi ke tempat kerjamu dari rumahmu?

Conversation 2

09.07 *Linda is at the mall, looking for the bathroom.*

1 What is on the right side of the cinema?

Linda	Permisi, kamu tahu di mana kamar kecil yang paling dekat?
Eva	Di lantai tiga.
Linda	Bagaimana cara pergi ke sana?
Eva	Kamu bisa naik eskalator, lift, atau tangga ke lantai tiga. WC umum di depan warnet.
Linda	Aku tidak tahu di mana warnet.
Eva	Warnet di samping kanan bioskop.
Linda	Maaf. Aku kurang tahu di mana itu.
Eva	Mari, aku antar kamu ke sana.
Linda	Tidak usah, terima kasih. Aku akan cari sendiri.
Eva	Tidak apa-apa. Aku juga perlu pergi ke atas.
Linda	Terima kasih. Maaf, aku merepotkan kamu.
Eva	Tidak apa-apa. Mari ikut aku.

lantai	*floor, level*
tangga	*staircase*
tidak usah	*no need to*
sendiri	*oneself*

While you have used the words **naik** and **turun** to talk about riding and getting on or off a mode of transport, they also mean, respectively, *ascend* and *descend*.

2 Find the expressions in the conversation that mean:

a How do I get there? _____

b I don't quite know where that is. _____

c There is no need to, thank you. _____

d Come follow me. _____

3 Check, then cover up your answers and see if you can say them without looking at the conversation.

4 Read or listen again and answer the questions.

a Where is the nearest bathroom?

b How can Linda get upstairs?

c What help does Eva offer her?

d What does Eva need to do?

5 09.08 Now listen to the lines from the conversation and repeat. Then listen to Eva's lines and respond as Linda.

Language discovery 2

Look at the sentences from the conversation. Put the words in English into Indonesian.

a Di (*third floor*).

b (*I*) akan cari (*myself*).

c (*No need to*), terima kasih.

1 NUMBERING AND NAMING FLOORS

In Indonesian, a **lantai** (*floor, level*) is not designated as first or second. Instead, **lantai satu** or **L1** is *floor one* meaning the *first floor*, which coincidentally is the *ground floor*, following American convention. The *second floor* is **lantai dua** or **L2**, and so on.

2 DOING SOMETHING ON YOUR OWN

The word **sendiri** (*oneself*) can be used after a verb to say that someone is doing something on their own.

Saya pergi sendiri. Dia mau cari sendiri.
I am going by myself. She wants to look for it on her own.

3 ACCEPTING AND REFUSING AN OFFER OF HELP

The phrase **tidak usah** (*no need to*) is often considered the opposite of the word **harus** (*must*). When someone offers to help you or do something for you, you can use **tidak usah** to say that there is *no need* for them to do it. It is also considered good manners to apologize for **merepotkan** (*imposing on, overburdening*) someone when accepting an offer of help.

Terima kasih, tetapi Anda tidak usah mengantar saya.

Thank you, but you do not need to escort me.

Maaf, saya merepotkan Anda.

Sorry, I am imposing on you.

Practice

1 **Put the following phrases into Indonesian.**
   - **a** first (*or* ground) floor
   - **b** second floor

2 **Put the following sentences into English.**
   - **a** Saya makan sendiri.
   - **b** Aku akan pulang sendiri.

3 **09.09 Practice accepting and refusing an offer to escort you somewhere.**

Listening

tanya	*ask, enquire*	**awas**	*beware (of)*
licin	*slippery*	**dilarang**	*forbidden*

1 09.10 **Justin gets lost whilst driving. Listen to the dialogue and answer the following questions.**

a Why does the woman tell Justin to park his car?
b Why does she tell him to be careful?
c What does the woman tell Justin he does not have to do?

The word **hati-hati** (*carefully*) can also mean *be careful.*

2 09.11 **Listen to the audio and match the places described to the locations on the map.**

apotek kantor pos rumah makan warnet apartemen kantor polisi alun-alun

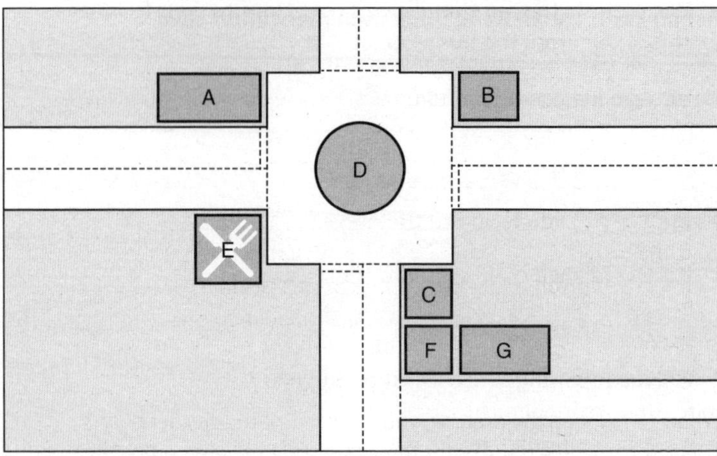

Reading and writing

1 Match the street signs to the relevant situations.

a trying to park during the day
b driving down a mountain pass
c trying to cross the street
d wanting to drop someone off

1 **2** **3** **4**

2 Write a text to your friends with directions to your favorite restaurant from the bus stop.

Teman-teman, turun bus di halte bus di depan ...

Go further

1 Match the Indonesian to the English.

a lantai atas	**1** *roundabout*
b lantai bawah	**2** *intersection*
c pertigaan	**3** *upper floor*
d perempatan	**4** *T-junction*
e bundaran	**5** *lower floor*

When completing the exercise, you might want to consider how a T-junction is where *three* paths meet. Similarly, an intersection is often where *four* paths meet. It might also be helpful to know that in an elevator or a lift in Indonesia, **LB** (lower basement) often marks a floor whose level is lower than ground level.

The **HI** (short for Hotel Indonesia) roundabout is a famous Jakarta landmark frequently featured in movies set in the city.

2 **Give the English for the following.**

a Aku turun eskalator pelan-pelan.

b Kamu menyeberang cepat-cepat.

c Ibu Dewi parkir hati-hati.

d Tolong ulang pelan-pelan.

In Indonesian, some adverbs or words describing the way an action is done, such as **pelan-pelan** (*slowly*) and **cepat-cepat** (*quickly*), are created by doubling an adjective such as **pelan** (*slow*) and **cepat** (*quick*). As in English, adverbs can come before or after the verb so that **hati-hati parkir** means *careful while parking* and **parkir hati-hati** means *park carefully*.

When someone is leaving or a party is breaking up, **Hati-hati, ya?** (*Be careful, all right?*) is often used in Indonesia as a goodbye to the person who will be journeying home or elsewhere.

3 **09.12 Read the questions below and prepare responses that are true for you. Then, listen and respond in real time. Do this as many times as you need to for it to become second nature.**

Bagaimana cara mengeja nama Anda?

Bagaimana cara pergi ke bandara dari rumah Anda?

Test yourself

1 Put the words in English into Indonesian.

(*How does one*) pergi ke masjid dari sini? (*Turn*) kiri dan jalan (*onwards*) sampai (*red light*), lalu (*turn right*) di (*intersection*). Kemudian (*cross*) jalan.

2 Use the words in the box to recreate the phrases below.

kedua terakhir anak pertama orang halte

a first (bus) stop
b last person
c second child

3 Match the Indonesian to the English.

a	di samping	**1**	*behind*
b	di antara	**2**	*across*
c	di belakang	**3**	*side*
d	di luar	**4**	*in front of*
e	di depan	**5**	*between*
f	di seberang	**6**	*outside*

4 Complete the sentences using the correct word.

a Tempat parkir di lantai *bawah / salah*.
b Loket karcis di lantai *dua / kedua*.
c Ibu bekerja di lantai *sebelah / atas* stasiun kereta baru.
d Kamar kecil di lantai *mana / berapa*, ya?

5 Give the English for the following.

a Saya tidak tinggal sendiri.
b Anisa bekerja sendiri di rumahnya.
c Mereka berjalan-jalan sendiri di Tebing Tinggi.
d Rosa akan pergi sendiri atau bersama kamu ke bandara?

6 Give the Indonesian for the following.

a Come, I will escort you.
b There is no need to, thank you.
c Please, Madam, follow me.
d Sorry, I am imposing on you.

SELF CHECK

	I CAN . . .
○	. . . ask for and understand directions.
○	. . . understand sequences using words and numbers.
○	. . . accept or refuse an offer of help.
○	. . . recognize warnings.
○	. . . ask and explain how to do something.

10

In this unit, you will learn how to:

- » talk about health complaints and parts of the body.
- » tell others how often you do something.
- » talk about time periods in relation to the present.
- » give and understand negative commands.
- » request appointments.

Semoga cepat sembuh!

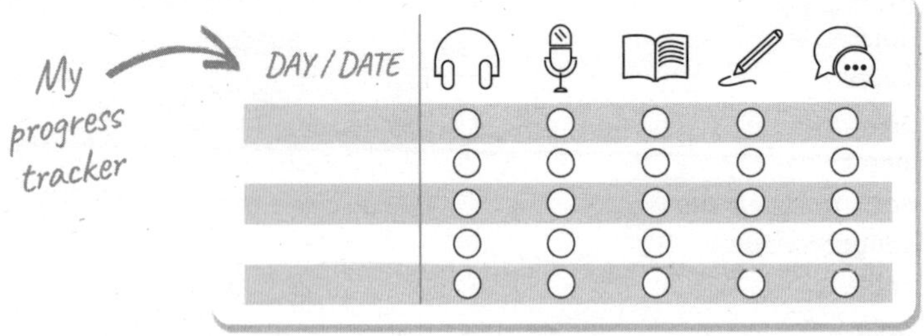

Health

When you **berlibur** (*are on vacation*) in tropical Indonesia, you'll probably have to watch your **kesehatan** (*health*) by being careful about the heat, sun, and humidity while your **badan** (*body*) adjusts. Having health insurance is uncommon in Indonesia and residents who are **takut** (*afraid of, nervous about*) becoming ill will try to avoid consuming food and drinks **sembarangan** (*carelessly*). If you **merasa tidak enak badan** (*feel unwell*), you can go to the pharmacy for over-the-counter **obat-obat** (*medicines*) or see a medical professional and obtain a **resep obat** (*prescription*). Most small communities benefit from access to a **puskesmas** (*public health clinic*) operated by doctors and **perawat-perawat** (*nurses*) employed by the government. In larger communities, there are doctors who **praktik** in private clinics, sometimes attached to their homes, and at the **rumah sakit** (*hospital*). It is common for a doctor to offer and attend **janji-janji** (*appointments*) in several locations. This could mean a longer waiting time for a **pasien** if the doctor has to travel through unexpectedly bad traffic that day. If you cannot wait, perhaps because you fear you've **menderita patah tulang** (*suffered a bone fracture*), you can go to the **UGD** or **Unit Gawat Darurat** (*Emergency Unit*).

What do you think **praktik** and **pasien** mean in English?

Vocabulary builder

1 10.01 Look at the words and phrases and complete the English translations. Then listen to the recording and imitate the pronunciation of the speakers.

HEALTH

luka	*wound, cut, injury*
sakit	*be ill, be sick, ache, hurt, pain*
sakit kepala	*(have a) headache*
kepala	________
sakit perut	*(have a) stomach ache*
perut	________
sakit tenggorokan	*(have a) sore throat*
tenggorokan	________
sakit kulit	*(have a) skin ailment*
kulit	________
dokter gigi	*dentist*
gigi	________
dokter umum	*general practitioner*
dokter anak	________

MEDICAL PROCEDURES

periksa	*to examine*
diperiksa	*to be examined*
ronsen	*x-ray*
dironsen	*to be x-rayed*
operasi	________
dioperasi	*to be operated on*

NEW EXPRESSIONS

ada	*to be present (somewhere)*
kenapa	*why*
karena	*because*
jatuh	*fall (down)*

sebaiknya	*it is best that ...*
jangan	*do not* (imperative)
khawatir	*worry*
lupa	*forget*
kali	*(number of) times/occasions*

2 10.02 Listen to the words about time, frequency, and other parts of the body and imitate the pronunciation of the speakers.

TIME

sejak	*since*
sampai	*until*
mulai	*to start*
sebelum	*before*
sesudah	*after*
lalu	*past*
depan	*ahead*
lusa	*day after tomorrow*

FREQUENCY

selalu	*always*
sering	*often*
biasanya	*usually*
jarang	*rarely*
tidak pernah	*never*

OTHER PARTS OF THE BODY

muka	*face*
telinga	*ear*
hidung	*nose*
mulut	*mouth*
leher	*neck*
bahu	*shoulder*
lengan	*arm*
siku	*elbow*
pergelangan tangan	*wrist*
tangan	*hand*
jari	*finger*
ibu jari	*thumb*
dada	*chest*
punggung	*back*
pinggul	*hip*

kaki *leg*
lutut *knee*
pergelangan kaki *ankle*
jari kaki *toe*

Conversation 1

10.03 *Linda arrives at a local doctor's practice where a nurse greets her.*

1 What is the matter with Linda?

Linda	Permisi. Pak Dokter ada?
Perawat	Pak Dokter sedang praktik di rumah sakit.
Linda	Sampai kapan Pak Dokter berada di sana?
Perawat	Dia berada di sana sampai jam enam. Ada apa, Bu? Kenapa cari Pak Dokter?
Linda	Karena saya mau minta janji dengan dia. Saya sakit kepala. Leher saya sakit juga. Saya ingin diperiksa oleh Pak Dokter.
Perawat	Sejak kapan kepala dan leher Ibu sakit?
Linda	Sejak minggu lalu. Sesudah saya jatuh pada hari Minggu sewaktu saya berlibur.
Perawat	Sejak tiga hari yang lalu, ya? Ada luka?
Linda	Tidak. Tidak ada luka.
Perawat	Sebaiknya Ibu diperiksa hari ini. Saya rasa Ibu perlu dironsen tetapi Pak Dokter akan lebih tahu.
Linda	Suster bisa buatkan janji untuk saya?
Perawat	Ya, Bu. Jangan khawatir. Saya akan menelpon rumah sakit dan meminta janji untuk Ibu.

oleh	*by*
rasa	*sense, feel*
lebih tahu	*know more/ better*
kadang-kadang	*sometimes*

A respectful way to address or refer to a doctor is to call him or her **Pak Dokter** or **Bu Dokter**. A **perawat** (*nurse*) is often called a **Suster** (*Sister*) due to the history of missionary service.

2 Find the expressions in the conversation that mean:

a What's the matter, Madam? ________
b Because I want to book an appointment with him. ________
c It is best that you're examined today. ________

3 **Read the text or listen again and answer the questions.**

a Is the doctor at the clinic?

b How long has Linda been in pain?

c What procedure does the nurse feel Linda will need?

4 **10.04 Now listen to the lines from the conversation and repeat. Be sure to pay attention to the pronunciation.**

Language discovery 1

Look at the sentences from the conversation. Put the words in English into Indonesian.

a Saya (*have a headache*). Leher saya (*hurts*) juga. Saya ingin (*be examined by*) Pak Dokter.

b Pak Dokter (*available*)? Dia (*is*) di sana sampai jam enam.

c Sejak (*last week*), pada hari Minggu. Sejak tiga hari (*ago*), ya?

d (*After*) saya jatuh pada hari Minggu sewaktu saya berlibur.

e (*Since*) kapan kepala dan leher Ibu sakit?

1 MEDICAL AILMENTS AND APPOINTMENTS

You've seen the word **sakit** (*ill, ache, hurt, pain*) used in Unit 3 so that **dia sakit** means *she was ill*. Here are its other uses.

Saya sakit gigi.	*I have a toothache.*
Gigi saya sakit.	*My tooth hurts.*
Saya merasa sakit.	*I feel ill* or *I feel pain.*

The word **luka** (*wound*) can be used in two ways.

Lengan saya luka.	*My arm is wounded.*
Ada luka di lengan saya.	*There is a wound on my arm.*

When you're discussing your medical ailments and treatments, the focus of conversation is you, your body, and how your body is the object of actions. In Indonesian, the focus of the sentence comes first. In medical situations, the passive voice is thus used frequently. For example, **saya dioperasi oleh dokter** (*I was operated on by the doctor*) is heard more frequently than **dokter mengoperasi saya** (*the doctor operated on me*).

An *appointment* with a doctor is a **janji** (lit. *promise*) and you would say, for example, **saya mau minta janji dengan dokter** (*I want to book/ request an appointment with the doctor*).

2 MORE ON THE VERB ADA

Recall that the word **ada** can be used to mean *to be available*. In this sense, it can also mean *to be present* somewhere. When the location is stated, you should use the **ber-** form, **berada**.

Apakah dokter ada?

Is the doctor in? Is the doctor available?

Dokter Umar berada di puskesmas.

Dokter Umar is (present) at the public health clinic.

3 PAST AND FUTURE TIME PERIODS

When you want to talk about specific days, weeks, months, and years, you can mention the time and describe how it is related to the present using **lalu** (*past*), **depan** (*ahead*), and **akan datang** (*will come*). There is also a particular word, **lusa**, that means *the day after tomorrow*.

tiga tahun yang lalu	*three years ago*
minggu lalu	*last week*
dua hari yang lalu	*two days ago*
tiga hari yang akan datang	*three days from now*
minggu depan	*next week*
dua bulan yang akan datang	*two months from now*

4 BEFORE AND AFTER

When you want to talk about events happening before or after a particular time period, you can use the words **sebelum** (*before*) or **sesudah** (*after*), as you would their English counterparts.

Kapan saya harus kembali? Seminggu sebelum operasi.

When must I return? A week before the operation.

Kapan aku akan diperiksa? Sesudah kamu dironsen.

When will I be examined? After you are x-rayed.

5 TALKING ABOUT WHEN SOMETHING BEGINS AND ENDS

You can use the word **sejak** (*since*) with time phrases to talk about when something began. However, if the beginning of the event is in the future, use **mulai dari** (*starting from*) instead.

Sejak kapan kamu demam? Sejak dua hari yang lalu.

Since when have you had the fever? Since two days ago.

Mulai dari kapan dia berlibur? Mulai dari bulan depan.

Starting from when is he on vacation? Starting from next month.

To talk about when an event ended or will end, you can use the word **sampai** (*until*).

Sampai kapan dada kamu sakit? Sampai minggu lalu.

Until when did your chest hurt? Until last week.

Sampai kapan Bu Dokter berada di sana? Sampai nanti sore.

Until when will the doctor be there? Until later this afternoon.

Practice

1 Put the following sentences into English.

- **a** Punggung saya sakit.
- **b** Kaki dan lutut saya luka.

2 Complete the sentences with *ada* **or** *berada.*

- **a** Maaf, Bu Dokter tidak. Saya berbicara dengan siapa?
- **b** Kapan Anda di Indonesia?

3 Put the following sentences into Indonesian.

- **a** A dancer was x-rayed five months ago.
- **b** You will be operated on next week.

4 Choose the correct word.

a	sesudah dioperasi	*before / after* being operated on
b	sebelum minum obat	*before / after* taking the medicine

5 10.05 Read the questions below and prepare responses that are true for you. Then, listen and respond in real time.

- **a** Sejak kapan Anda belajar bahasa Indonesia?
- **b** Mulai dari kapan Anda berlibur?

Pronunciation

10.06 You might hear *kh* **pronounced similarly to** *ch* **in the English word** *loch* **or as the letter** *k***. Listen to how the following words are pronounced and repeat.**

1 khas	**3** khawatir
2 khitanan	**4** khusus

Speaking

10.07 You are a patient phoning the doctor's to make an appointment. Prepare your responses to the following questions. Then, listen and respond in real time.

Resepsionis	Bisa saya bantu?
Pasien	*Say you want to book an appointment with your chosen medical professional.*
Resepsionis	Untuk hari apa?
Pasien	*Make a choice to suit your schedule.*
Resepsionis	Saya bisa buatkan janji untuk sore hari. Anda bisa datang pada jam berapa?
Pasien	*Make a choice to suit your schedule.*

Conversation 2

10.08 *Jon is being examined by a doctor.*

1 What does the doctor tell Jon not to do?

Dokter	Sejak kapan Pak Jon merasa tidak enak badan?
Jon	Sejak dua hari yang lalu. Saya sakit perut dan muntah setiap hari.
Dokter	Anda sering atau jarang harus pergi ke WC?
Jon	Saya sering harus pergi ke WC.
Dokter	Apakah Anda selalu makan hati-hati?
Jon	Tidak selalu. Saya kadang-kadang makan sembarangan. Dan saya sering lupa makan.
Dokter	Sesudah ini, tolong jangan makan sembarangan. Ini resep obat antibiotik. Anda harus minum obat ini tiga kali sehari. Obatnya harus diminum sampai habis.
Jon	Di mana saya bisa membeli obatnya?
Dokter	Anda bisa menebus resepnya di apotek.

muntah	*to vomit*
tebus	*to redeem*
habis	*have run out, be finished*

2 Find the expressions in the conversation that mean:

- **a** take this medicine ________
- **b** antibiotic prescription ________
- **c** buy the medicine ________
- **d** redeem the prescription ________

3 Check, then cover up your answers and see if you can say them without looking at the conversation.

4 Read or listen to the text again and answer the following questions.

- **a** Since when has Jon been feeling ill?
- **b** What symptoms does Jon have?
- **c** What are Jon's eating habits?
- **d** Where can Jon redeem the prescription?

5 10.09 Now listen to the lines from the conversation and repeat. Then listen to the doctor's lines and respond as Jon.

Language discovery 2

Look at the sentences from the conversation. Put the words in English into Indonesian.

- **a** Anda harus minum obat ini (*three times a day*).
- **b** Sesudah ini, (*do not*) makan sembarangan.
- **c** Dan saya (*often forget to eat*).

1 HOW MANY TIMES ...?

Whenever you saw the phrase **sekali lagi** (*once more*) perhaps you had the idea that **sekali** could be another way of saying **satu kali** (*one time*). That would be correct! To say *three times a day*, you would therefore say **tiga kali sehari**. The question you'd ask is **Berapa kali sehari?** (*How many times a day?*)

> Along with **tiga kali sehari** (*three times a day*), you might hear Indonesian speakers reverse the order and say **sehari tiga kali** (*in one day, three times*).

2 DON'T ...

To tell people not to do something, use the word **jangan** (*do not*). You can also say **tolong jangan** (*please do not*).

Jangan makan sembarangan. *Don't eat carelessly.*

Tolong jangan khawatir. *Please don't worry.*

3 TALKING ABOUT HABITS USING FREQUENCY WORDS

You can talk about how rarely or often you do something by using a frequency word such as **jarang** (*rarely*) or **sering** (*often*), which you place before the verb. When you negate the combination, place **tidak** (*not*) before the combination.

Kamu sering sakit? *Are you often ill?*

Tidak. Aku tidak sering sakit. *No. I'm not often ill.*

Practice

1 Give the Indonesian sentences for the following.

- **a** I practice at the hospital four times a week.
- **b** My skin is examined once a year.

2 Unscramble the words to make full sentences.

- **a** janji - lupa - dokter - Tolong - Anda - dengan - jangan!
- **b** makan - dironsen - Anda - sebelum - Jangan.

3 10.10 Read the questions below and prepare responses that are true for you. Then, listen and respond in real time.

- **a** Kamu sering berlibur?
- **b** Anda biasanya makan di mana?

Listening

kecelakaan	*accident,* (coll.) *have an accident*
ambulans	*ambulance*
Tidak ada apa-apa.	*Nothing's the matter.*
Semoga cepat sembuh.	*Get well soon.*

1 10.11 Ani has returned from the public health clinic after receiving treatment for a minor accident. Ani's mother is worried about her. Listen to the dialogue and answer the following questions.

- **a** What did Ani do that was unusual, according to her mother?
- **b** Where is she injured and did she need an x-ray?
- **c** When does Ani have to return to the clinic?

2 10.12 **Listen to the patients being interviewed and match the names to the ailments. Then, listen again and respond by wishing him/her a speedy recovery in real time.**

a Tuti	*toothache*
b Ian	*hip bone fracture*
c Siti	*influenza*

From what you know about the word **perawat** (*nurse*), you may have recognized that to **rawat** others is to *nurse* or *care for* them. If you see signs for **rawat inap** and **rawat jalan** in an Indonesian hospital, you would also be correct in thinking they mean, respectively, *inpatient care* and *outpatient care*.

Reading and writing

1 Anisa has written an email to Harjeet after hearing that he was in hospital. Read her email.

New message

Harjeet,

Apa kabar? Kakakmu menelpon aku tadi malam dari Eropa. Dia bilang kamu kecelakaan dan menderita patah tulang bulan lalu, kemudian kamu dirawat inap di rumah sakit selama dua minggu. Dia juga bilang sesudah itu kamu boleh pulang ke Wales, tetapi kamu harus kembali ke rumah sakit sekali seminggu untuk diperiksa oleh dokter dan dirawat jalan. Bahu kamu masih sakit? Semoga cepat sembuh, Harjeet! Aku tunggu kabarmu.

Salam hangat,
Anisa

2 Imagine your friend is recovering from an illness or injury. Write an email to wish them a speedy recovery.

Go further

Here are some other useful words:

hamil — *to be pregnant*
kursi roda — *wheelchair*
sakit flu — *(have) the flu*

When you saw **tidak pernah** (*never*) used to talk about habits, you probably also considered the meaning of **pernah**.

1 Put the following into English. Think carefully.

a Saya tidak pernah belajar.
b Saya pernah belajar bahasa Indonesia.

One of the words used in Indonesian to discuss when things happened, **pernah** is used to talk about whether something has *ever* happened before so that in a sentence **pernah** can be thought of as *have ... before*.

Saya pernah sakit flu. I have had the flu before.

Indonesian speakers also use **belum pernah** to mean *have never yet* and **sudah pernah** to mean *already have ... before*.

Saya belum pernah hamil. I've never yet been pregnant.
Saya sudah pernah hamil. I've already been pregnant before.

If you want to say, for example, that you (*never have the flu*) because influenza never troubles you, you would say you **tidak pernah sakit flu.** However, if you want to say that you *have never yet had the flu before* in your lifetime, you would say you **belum pernah sakit flu.**

When people know you are studying Indonesian, they are more likely to ask if you **sudah pernah pergi ke Indonesia** (*have already gone to Indonesia before*) than to ask if you **pernah pergi ke Indonesia** (*have gone to Indonesia before*) because there is an expectation that you have already made a trip there or that you'll be making a trip there if you haven't yet done so.

2 10.13 Read the questions below and prepare your own responses. Then, listen and respond in real time.

a Sampai kapan kamu belajar bahasa Indonesia?
b Kamu kadang-kadang perlu kursi roda?
c Kamu sudah pernah berlibur di Indonesia?

Test yourself

1 Put the words in English into Indonesian.

Bulan lalu, keponakan saya (*had a stomach ache*). Orang tuanya (*requested an appointment with*) dokter anak. Dia (*was examined*) hari itu juga. Pak Dokter memberikan dia (*drug prescription*). Sesudah keponakan saya (*took that medicine*), dia (*felt*) lebih baik. (Since) itu, dia makan hati-hati.

2 Unscramble the words to make full sentences.

a Jon? - apa, - ada - Pak - Maaf,
b puskesmas. - berada - Perawat-perawat - di
c ada? - Dokter - Bu
d di - berada - tunggu? - kamar - Siapa

3 Match the Indonesian phrases to the English.

a dua minggu yang lalu	**1** *two weeks from now*
b minggu depan	**2** *two weeks ago*
c dua minggu yang akan datang	**3** *next week*

4 Put the following sentences into English.

a Tolong minum obat sesudah makan malam.
b Lusa Anda akan dironsen sebelum diperiksa oleh dokter.
c Pergelangan kaki saya sakit sebelum saya dioperasi.

5 Choose the correct word.

a sampai tahun lalu	*until / since* last year
b sejak saya jatuh	*until / since* I fell down

6 Put the following sentences into Indonesian.

a How many times a week?
b Drink this medicine three times a day.
c The nurse comes once every hour.

7 Complete the sentences to give negative commands.

a ________ takut. Ini tidak sakit.
b ________ minum obat sembarangan.
c ________ ________ lupa belajar bahasa Indonesia.

8 Put the words in English into Indonesian.

a Keluarga Lim (*are often on vacation*) di Kanada.
b Saya (*not often*) sakit kepala.
c Pasien-pasien (*are never examined*) bersama.
d Jari-jari Affandi (*are always hurting*).

SELF CHECK

	I CAN ...
○	... talk about health complaints and parts of the body.
○	... tell others how often I do something.
○	... talk about time periods in relation to the present.
○	... give and understand negative commands.
○	... ask for appointments.

R3 Review 3

1 Put the following everyday expressions into Indonesian.

a What time is it now?
b Which one is the fastest train?
c Is there a table for six people?
d Enjoy your meal.
e The check, please.
f May I ask ...
g How do I go by bus to the supermarket?
h Please repeat slowly.
i Sorry that I am imposing on you.
j Don't forget.

2 Match the questions and statements to the replies.

a Berapa ongkos perjalanan?	**1** Selamat tinggal.
b Berapa lama perjalanan?	**2** Tidak ada apa-apa.
c Selamat jalan.	**3** Tiga puluh ribu rupiah.
d Silakan duduk.	**4** Tidak usah.
e Saya antar Anda ke sana.	**5** Enam jam.
f Ada apa?	**6** Terima kasih.

3 Pingkan keeps a travel journal. Read the entry about her recent trip home and answer the questions that follow.

Pagi ini dingin. Aku naik bus dari Batu lalu ganti kendaraan di Malang. Kereta jurusan Surabaya berangkat dari stasiun pada jam setengah lima sore. Harga tiketnya seratus sembilan puluh ribu. Sesudah dua jam duduk di dalam kereta, aku sampai di Surabaya. Di stasiun tidak ada ojek jadi aku naik taksi dan terkena macet. Aku terlambat tetapi makan malam di rumah keluargaku masih hangat. Sopnya enak sekali. Aku rasa ibuku tahu aku akan terlambat. Minggu depan aku harus kembali ke Batu. Sebelum itu, aku akan sibuk bermain bersama keponakan-keponakanku dan makan masakan ibu.

a Was the morning warm or cold?
b What time did the train leave and how long was the trip?
c What transport option was and was not available in Surabaya?
d Where did Pingkan have dinner and how was the food?
e When does she have to return to Batu?
f What will keep her busy before she returns to Batu?

4 Match the Indonesian to the English.

a dilarang parkir	1 *do not stop here*
b dilarang menyeberang	2 *beware of slippery sidewalk*
c awas trotoar licin	3 *no parking*
d jangan berhenti di sini	4 *do not walk here*
e jangan berjalan di sini	5 *no crossing*

5 Give the following in English.

a jam tujuh kurang seperempat pagi
b jam tiga lewat sepuluh menit siang
c semangkok bubur nasi ayam yang tidak pedas
d segelas es kopi susu
e dua botol air mineral
f pasien kedelapan

6 Ian and Ying are at a street stall. She's picking up a takeaway while he's having a drink and waiting for his food. Read their conversation and answer the questions that follow.

Ian	Ying, kamu pesan apa untuk dibawa pulang?
Ying	Aku pesan empat porsi sate kambing, dua porsi lontong, dan dua porsi nasi goreng telur pedas.
Ian	Kamu bisa makan semua makanan itu?
Ying	Ini pesanan keluargaku dan kami lapar.
Ian	Oh begitu. Mereka suka makanan yang pedas, ya? Aku suka yang pedas juga. Aku baru pesan mie rebus pedas dan ayam bakar lada hitam.
Ying	Ayam bakarnya enak. Kamu minum apa?
Ian	Ini es susu kedelai manis. Kamu mau coba?
[Ian motions for the vendor to come over.]	
Ian	Pak, satu es susu kedelai manis lagi!
Ying	Tidak usah, Ian, terima kasih.
Ian	Tidak apa-apa, Ying. Cobalah.
Ying	Berapa, Pak? Aku mau bayar sendiri.

- **a** What did Ying order and why did she order so much food?
- **b** What kind of food does Ian like?
- **c** What did Ian just order to eat and what does Ying say about it?
- **d** What does Ian order after getting the vendor to come over?
- **e** How would you order the same but ask for it to be served *not sweet* or *without sugar*?
- **f** What does Ying say to the vendor?

7 Unscramble the words to make complete sentences.

- **a** tanah. - beralergi - Saya - kacang.
- **b** kamar - ke - mengantar - Perawat - saya - kecil.
- **c** garpu. -ambilkan - Tolong - sendok.
- **d** suka - tidak - goreng - yang - Saya - asin. - kentang.
- **e** mau - umum. - Hitomi - janji - dokter - dengan - minta.

8 Look at the English translations, then choose the correct word to complete the Indonesian phrases.

a	saya *haus / kenyang*	I am thirsty
b	*kecap / saos* manis	sweet soy sauce
c	*lusa / lalu*	the day after tomorrow
d	bulan *lusa / lalu*	last month
e	tumis *tahu / tahun*	stir-fried tofu
f	kepiting *asam / asin* manis	sweet-and-sour crab

9 Pak Rusli has taken notes about a house that he's thinking of moving into with his family. Complete his notes by putting the words in English into Indonesian.

- (*not far*) dari bandar udara
- ada (*market*) yang (near)
- ada (*crosswalk*) di setiap (*traffic light*)
- ada halte bus (*across the street from*) sekolah
- di mal ada (*pharmacy on the 3rd floor*)
- rumah (*between*) rumah sakit dan kantor
- (*on the upper floor*), kamar tidur (*next to*) ruang duduk
- ada halaman besar (*behind*) rumah

10 Give the root of the words in parentheses.

a Kamu belum pernah makan (makanan) Indonesia?
b Dokter (memeriksa) saya karena saya sakit tenggorokan.
c Wartawan itu (dioperasi) dua minggu yang akan datang.
d Tolong hati-hati kalau Anda (merasa) pusing.
e Dokter (menekan) pergelangan tangan ibuku.
f Mereka (mengantar) adik mereka ke puskesmas.

11 Choose the correct word.

a *Sejak / Belum* kapan kamu bekerja di perusahaan swasta?
b *Sudah / Sampai* kapan Anda berada di sana?
c Mulai *dari / ke* kapan Jon tinggal di Indonesia?
d Berapa *kali / kalian* setahun kamu berlibur di Inggris?
e *Kalian / Kali* mau minum apa?
f *Ada / Berada* dokter anak?

12 Bima has written an email to Ian's parents describing their son's life as a boarder in his house. Complete the excerpt by putting the words in Indonesian into English.

New message

a (Yth.) Mr and Mrs Park,

b (*Dua bulan yang lalu*), your son Ian **c** (*mulai*) studying at the university. He will be **d** (*seorang wartawan*) we will all admire. He **e** (*selalu*) studies hard and **f** (*kadang-kadang*) forgets to eat. He **g** (*jarang*) sleeps early. When I asked him **h** (*kenapa*), he **i** (*berkata*) it's **j** (*karena*) he **k** (*tidak pernah*) knows when to stop. Ian **l** (*merasa tidak enak badan*) last week. The doctor said Ian **m** (*sakit flu*). We all wished he would **n** (*cepat sembuh*). He **o** (*dia minum obat empat kali sehari*). This week, **p** (*kesehatan anak Anda*) is better. I will **q** (*hubungi*) you again **r** (*tiga hari yang akan datang*) to give you an update. I hope you are all well there. My family and I wish you a **s** '(*Selamat Tahun Baru*)!'

With thanks,

Bima

13 ***Selamat ulang tahun, Pak Jon!*** **Linda and Saul are throwing Jon a birthday party. They want to give the guests the directions to their house. Use the words in the box to complete the Indonesian translations.**

> jalan lurus terus, turn, ada, naik, Kalau, kira-kira, delapan puluh delapan, sembilan puluh sembilan, Masuk, perempatan, Terakhir, pertama, sesudah, Belok kiri, caranya

New message

Friends, **the way** is this: **first, get on** bus number **ninety-nine**, then **get off** the bus at Kenanga Street. **Enter** that street and walk for **roughly** five minutes until Merak Street. **If** you can't see the street name, at the **intersection** of Kenanga Street and Merak Street **there is** a dental clinic. **Turn left** at that intersection. Then **keep walking straight** down the road. Turn right **after** the mosque. **Finally**, look for house number **eighty-eight.** See you at our house!

New message

Teman-teman, __________ begini: __________, __________ bus nomor __________, lalu __________ bus di Jalan Kenanga. __________ jalan itu dan jalan kaki selama __________ lima menit sampai Jalan Merak. __________ kamu tidak bisa lihat nama jalannya, di __________ Jalan Kenanga dan Jalan Merak __________ klinik dokter gigi. __________ di persimpangan itu. Kemudian __________. Belok kanan __________ masjid. __________, cari rumah nomor __________. Sampai jumpa di rumah kami!

Grammar guide

Here are a few fundamental grammar points that you can review whenever you need to get your bearings.

Word order

The word order in Indonesian sentences does not differ much from the word order in English sentences; for example, **saya makan jeruk** (*I eat an orange*) and **jeruk dimakan oleh saya** (*the orange was eaten by me*). However, an Indonesian noun phrase is the reverse of what an English noun phrase would be so that *my left foot* would be **kaki kiri saya**. Depending on word order, moreover, a pronoun such as **saya** (*I*) can also work as a possessive such as *my* so that **topi saya** is *my hat*. Verbal phrases are in the same order as they are in English so that *not still sleeping* would be **tidak masih tidur**.

Words

Some Indonesian words share the same beginnings and endings. This is because Indonesian words can be developed out of root words using affixes (whether prefixes, suffixes, or both), which are word parts attached to the beginning or end of a word. Here are some affixes and examples of their use

- -an is a suffix used to form a noun so that **makan** (*to eat*) becomes **makanan** (*food*).
- ber- is a prefix used to form an active verb so that **main** (*to play*) becomes **bermain** (*play*) and **sepeda** (*bicycle*) becomes **bersepeda** (*cycle, ride a bicycle*).
- di- is a prefix used to form a passive verb so that **periksa** (*to examine*) becomes **diperiksa** (*to be examined*).
- meX-, where X stands for a consonant that changes depending on the first letter of the root word, is a prefix used to form an active verb

so that **periksa** (*to examine*) becomes **memeriksa** (*examine*). In general meX- verbs are used when the action involves someone or something else. For example, you **mendengar** (*hear*) a sound and you **memeriksa** (*examine*) a patient.

- pe- or peX- are prefixes that are used to make an actor out of a verb or action word so that a **pekerja** (*worker*) is someone who **kerja** (*works*).

Questions

You can form Indonesian questions in the way you would form statements or in the way you would form questions in English. A question can be posed as **Apa ini?** (*What is this?*) or as **Ini apa?** (*This is what?*), which has the same word order as the statement **Ini topi.** (*This is a hat.*) In a question that is ordered like a statement, the question word, in this case **apa** (*what*), is placed where the unknown information would be in the answer. Any question involving numbers must be asked using **berapa** (*how many*), whether the answer is a date, a time, or an amount.

Situating actions in time

Verbs do not change according to when actions happen since there are no tenses in Indonesian. To situate an action in time, use words and phrases such as **tadi** (*earlier*), **nanti** (*later*), **jam tiga sore** (*3 p.m.*), **kemarin** (*yesterday*), **hari ini** (*today*), **besok** (*tomorrow*), and so on. You can also use temporal markers to say, for example, whether an action **pernah** (*ever*) happened or **akan** (*will*) happen. Here are some other markers:

baru	*recently, just*	**masih**	*still*
belum	*not yet*	**sudah**	*already*

Location

Whenever something or someone *is* somewhere, you must use the location word **di** (*at/in/on*); for example, **dia duduk di sini** (*he sits here*) and **dia bermain di luar** (*she plays outside*).

Counting

Indonesian speakers might use classifiers when counting things so that, for example, people are counted in **orang**, animals are counted in **ekor**, and large things are counted in **buah**. You say **dua orang anak** (*two children*) when counting with classifiers and **dua anak** (*two children*) when counting without them.

References

Sneddon, J.N. (2010) *Indonesian: A Comprehensive Grammar* 2nd Edition. London: Routledge.

Stevens, A.M. & Schmidgall-Tellings A., ed. (2004) *A Comprehensive Indonesian–English Dictionary*. Athens: Ohio University Press.

Answer key

Unit 1

INDONESIAN

Europe, Japan, phone, university, accountant, doctor

VOCABULARY BUILDER

Greetings
morning, afternoon, evening

CONVERSATION 1

1 Jakarta
2 a 4 Where do you live? **b 3** Excuse me. **c 1** Until we meet again.
d 2 Where do you come from?
3 a between 3 p.m. and 6 p.m., **b** Liverpool, **c** University of Palembang,
d colleague

LANGUAGE DISCOVERY 1

a Ini Jonathan Curtis. Saya Budi. **b** Di mana Anda bekerja? Saya kerja di universitas. **c** Dari mana Anda berasal? Anda tinggal di mana?

PRACTICE

1 a Bahasa Inggris bahasa ibu saya. **b** Saya bekerja di kantor. **c** Ini kolega saya. **d** Utomo tinggal di Cina.
2 a 3 kerja, **b 1** temu, **c 4** asal, **d 2** bahasa
3 Model answers:
a Saya berasal dari India. **b** Saya tinggal di Korea. **c** Saya bekerja di hotel di Skotlandia. **d** Nama bank saya Bank Indonesia.

SPEAKING

Model answers:
a Saya Patricia Smith. **b** Kenalkan. Ini Wati. **c** Kolega saya berasal dari Malaysia.

CONVERSATION 2

1 Hotel Indonesia

2 a Siapa nama kamu? **b** Apa itu? **c** Terima kasih. **d** Sama-sama.

4 a Siti, **b** England, **c** Linda, **d** informal

5 Hotel Indonesia. Sama-sama. Dah, Bu Linda!

LANGUAGE DISCOVERY 2

a Siapa, **b** apa

PRACTICE

1 a Siapa nama Anda/kamu? **b** Apa nama universitas itu? **c** Linda orang Inggris.

2 Model answers:

Kamu orang apa, Chris?, Aku orang Kanada. Dan kamu? Aku orang Australia., Orang apa kamu, Peter?, Aku orang Singapura.

LISTENING

1 a 3 01:30 p.m. **b 4** 05:00 p.m. **c 2** 06:00 a.m. **d 1** 11:00 p.m.

2 Heryanto, Indonesia, Scotland, University of Aberdeen, Mimi, USA, England, University of London

3 Model answers:

a Nama aku James. **b** Aku tinggal di Selandia Baru sekarang. **c** Aku berasal dari Hong Kong.

READING AND WRITING

1 a Alex orang Indonesia. **b** Alex berasal dari Sulawesi. **c** Alex tinggal di Cardiff sekarang. **d** Alex bekerja dan belajar di Universitas Wales.

GO FURTHER

1 a 5 Javanese, **b 3** Sundanese, **c 4** Malay, **d 1** Madurese, **e 2** Batak

2 Model answers:

a Pramoedya Ananta Toer orang Jawa. Pramoedya Ananta Toer orang Indonesia. **b** Saya/Aku belajar bahasa Indonesia.

TEST YOURSELF

1 a 2 11:00 a.m., **b 4** 05:00 p.m., **c 1** 09:00 a.m., **d 3** 11:00 p.m.

2 a Where do you work? **b** I work at a university. **c** Bambang works in Japan.

3 a di, **b** dari, **c** ke

4 a Siapa, **b** Apa, **c** Siapa, **d** apa

5 a Saya/aku orang Skotlandia. **b** Kolega saya orang Selandia Baru. **c** Anda orang apa? **d** Ibu/Bu Rosa berasal dari mana?

Unit 2

COMMUNITY

bermain sepak bola

VOCABULARY BUILDER

Adjectives
old, short

CONVERSATION 1

1 They went scuba diving.
2 a Saya tetangga baru Anda. **b** Siapa dia? **c** Dia senang apa? **d** Ayo!
4 a evening, **b** no, **c** Linda and Affandi, **d** introduce Affandi to Linda

LANGUAGE DISCOVERY 1

a teman lama saya, **b** Kita, Kami **c** bukan, tidak

PRACTICE

1 a my new acquaintance, **b** our short friend, **c** our old neighbor
2 a Kita, **b** Kami
3 Model answers:
a Apakah Anda berlatih pencak silat di Indonesia? Tidak. Saya tidak berlatih pencak silat di Indonesia. **b** Apakah Anda orang Indonesia? Bukan. Saya bukan orang Indonesia. **c** Apakah Anda tinggi? Tidak. Saya tidak tinggi.

SPEAKING

Model answers:
Dia Kazuo. Dia orang Jepang. Dia tinggi. Kami senang berenang, bermain bulu tangkis, dan makan-makan.
Dia Julia. Dia orang Amerika. Dia pendek. Kami senang menari di kampung, membaca, dan minum-minum.

CONVERSATION 2

1 081174625329
2 a 3 earlier this morning, **b 4** now, **c 2** later this afternoon, **d 1** later tonight
3 a earlier this morning, **b** later tonight, **c** later this afternoon, **d** daytime (between 10 a.m. and 3 p.m.)
4 Nomor ponsel saya kosong – delapan – satu – satu – tujuh – empat – enam – dua – lima – tiga – dua – sembilan., Ya. Itu nomor ponsel saya., Sampai nanti sore.

LANGUAGE DISCOVERY 2

a tadi pagi, **b** Berapa, Pak Jon

PRACTICE

1 a Saya bermain musik tradisional tadi pagi dan tadi malam. **b** Tadi siang, dia dan Budi bermain catur.

2 Model answers:

Berapa nomor telepon Anda? Nomor telepon saya kosong – dua – tujuh – tiga – lima – tiga – empat – delapan – kosong – sembilan., Berapa nomor telepon Rachel? Nomor telepon saya nol – delapan – satu – satu – enam – empat – dua – lima – tiga – tujuh – lima.

LISTENING

1 a in the school yard, **b** on the porch, **c** later this evening

2 HP: 07798681434, kantor 041390572, rumah 0419903416

3 Model answers:

a Tidak. Teman saya tidak muda. Dia tua. **b** Saya harus membaca sekarang. **c** Nomor telepon aku tujuh-nol-tujuh-lima-nol-satu-sembilan.

READING AND WRITING

2 Model answer:

Halo dari Indonesia! Eko teman baru saya. Dia orang Indonesia. Dia berasal dari Ponorogo. Kami bertemu di universitas. Dia belajar bahasa Inggris dan saya belajar bahasa Indonesia. Dia ramah dan pendek. Tadi pagi kami belajar di rumah dia. Sampai nanti!

GO FURTHER

1 a Saya senang. **b** Bermain gamelan menyenangkan. **c** Saya senang pergi ke Indonesia.

2 Model answers:

a Ya. Musik tradisional negara saya menyenangkan., Tidak. Musik tradisional negara saya tidak menyenangkan. **b** Ya. Bertemu orang Indonesia menyenangkan., Tidak. Bertemu orang Indonesia tidak menyenangkan.

TEST YOURSELF

1 a Dia tetangga baru saya. **b** Ini nomor telepon rumah dia. **c** Itu halaman sekolah kamu/Anda.

2 a Kita, **b** Kami, **c** Kita

3 a Tidak, tidak, **b** tidak, **c** Bukan, bukan

4 a 2 earlier this afternoon, **b 3** later this afternoon, **c 4** last night, **d 1** later this evening

5 a number, **b** cell phone, **c** What is your handphone number?
6 a Ke mana aku dan Linda pergi sekarang? **b** Di mana dia bertemu Linda nanti? **c** Linda dan beliau berselam skuba di mana?

Unit 3

FAMILY

keluarga-keluarga

VOCABULARY BUILDER

Family members
younger siblings, older siblings, grandchildren

CONVERSATION 1

1 Jon
2 a Kasihan! **b** Apa kabar? **c** Bagus! **d** Apa kabar keluarga Anda?
4 a early afternoon, **b** Budi's wife, **c** three, **d** Jon's elder brother's family.

LANGUAGE DISCOVERY 1

1 a baik, **b** baik, **c** Bagus
2 a Saya belum menikah. **b** Mereka sudah punya cucu-cucu.

PRACTICE

1 a How are you? **b** I am well. **c** How are they?
2 a Sudah. Saya sudah menikah., Belum. Saya belum menikah. **b** Sudah. Saya sudah punya cucu., Belum. Saya belum punya cucu.

SPEAKING

1 Model answers:
Siti dan Harmoko orang tua Ina. Edwin kakek Rudi. Mutia nenek Ratna. Ina ibu Rudi dan Bastian. Lina dan Ratna anak-anak perempuan Hendri dan Ina. Rudi, Bastian, Lina, dan Ratna cucu-cucu Edwin dan Mutia. Bastian saudara laki-laki Lina. Ratna saudara perempuan Rudi. Hendri suami Ina. Ina istri Hendri.

CONVERSATION 2

1 Jon's younger brother
2 a Jon was still working, **b** two, **c** repeat one more time, **d** that Budi will call Jon tomorrow

3 a 4 Can I speak to Mr Jon? **b 3** I don't understand. **c 2** Can I leave a message? **d 1** All right.
4 Saya tidak mengerti. Tolong ulang sekali lagi., Saya mengerti sekarang. Apa pesan Anda?, Baiklah., Sama-sama.

LANGUAGE DISCOVERY 2
a Saya menelpon dia besok. **b** dua adik, **c** Tolong bilang, 'Saya mengerti sekarang.'

PRACTICE
1 a Saya menelpon kakak laki-laki saya kemarin. **b** Saya menelpon adik perempuan saya hari ini. **c** Saya sampaikan pesan Anda/kamu besok.
2 a anak, **b** kantor-kantor
3 Model answers:
Bisa titip pesan?, Apa pesan Anda?, Tolong bilang, 'Kita belajar bahasa Indonesia hari ini.', Baiklah. Nanti saya sampaikan., Terima kasih., Sama-sama.

LISTENING
1 a yes, **b** yes, **c** her husband's parents' house
2 grandfather and grandmother are going to Jakarta later this afternoon, grandmother
3 Model answers:
a Kabar baik. **b** Mereka baik. **c** Ya. Saya mengerti sedikit bahasa Indonesia.

READING AND WRITING
2 Model answer:
Apa kabar? Apa kabar orang tua kamu?
Kabar saya dan orang tua saya baik. Kami tinggal di Aberdeen, Skotlandia. Saya punya satu adik laki-laki. Dia tinggal di Glasgow. Kakek saya berasal dari Irlandia. Saya senang bicara dengan sepupu-sepupu saya di Waterford. Saya juga punya saudara di Amerika dan di Inggris.

GO FURTHER
1 Model answers:
a Tidak. Saya tidak punya banyak saudara., Ya. Saya punya banyak saudara. **b** Bisa. Saya bisa bicara bahasa Indonesia., Bisa. Sedikit.

TEST YOURSELF
1 a Apa kabar? **b** Kabar baik. Dan Anda? **c** Saya baik juga. **d** Bagus!
2 a 3 already married, **b 1** not yet married, **c 2** still married
3 a belum, hari ini, **b** sudah, kemarin, **c** masih, **d** Besok

4 a rumah-rumah, **b** lima keluarga, **c** delapan anak
5 a pass on, message, **b** say, **c** understand, **d** Please repeat once more. / Please repeat one more time.

R1

1 a Selamat pagi, **b** Selamat siang, **c** Selamat sore, **d** Selamat malam
2 a saya, aku, **b** Anda, kamu, **c** dia, **d** kita, kami, **e** mereka
3 a Terima kasih. **b** Sama-sama. **c** Permisi. **d** Sampai bertemu lagi. **e** Bisa bicara dengan Ibu Taraji?
4 a siapa, **b** Dari mana, **c** Di mana, **d** Apa, **e** ke mana
5 a Ini, bekerja (*or* kerja), **b** Itu, tinggi, teman, orang Inggris, bahasa Indonesia, **c** senang, **d** tetangga baru Linda, orang Indonesia, kenal, **e** tinggal, Kakek dia, dari
6 a Bukan. Dia bukan orang Selandia Baru. **b** Tidak. Mereka tidak berlatih pencak silat tadi siang. **c** Tidak. Suami saya tidak pendek. **d** Tidak. Saya tidak menelpon orang tua saya.
7 a 5 I don't understand. **b 1** Please repeat once more. **c 4** Can I leave a message? **d 3** What is your message? **e 2** I will pass it on.
8 a What is Anisa's (*or* your) phone number? **b** My phone number is seven-two-five-six-zero-four-one-nine. **c** I have eight children. My children live in Solo. **d** How many are your siblings (*or* How many siblings do you have)? **e** My siblings are three in number (*or* I have three siblings).
9 a sudah belajar tadi pagi, **b** masih bekerja nanti, **c** belum punya anak
10 a 3 Kabar baik. **b 4** Bagus! **c 2** Kasihan! **d 1** Tolong bilang ...
11 a has not eaten yet, **b** aunt, last night, **c** at home
12 a Suteja's younger brother Koes, **b** his grandparents, his cousin, and himself, **c** yesterday, **d** played traditional Sudanese music with his grandfather on the porch

Unit 4

DAILY LIFE
makan siang

VOCABULARY BUILDER

Days of the week
Friday, Sunday

Numbers
30, 31, 90, 99

CONVERSATION 1

1 At the weekend
2 a Thursday, **b** she is a civil servant, **c** sixteen years old, **d** yes
3 a 4 Hari ini hari Kamis. **b 3** Sampai nanti! **c 2** Tidak apa-apa. **d 1** Dia pergi pada hari Selasa.
5 Hari ini hari Kamis., Oh, tidak apa-apa. Apa pekerjaan dia?, Kapan dia pergi?, Siapa memasak di rumah minggu ini?, Oh begitu. Berapa umur anak Pak Frans?, Oh ya, Pak Frans sudah makan siang?, Baiklah. Sampai nanti!

LANGUAGE DISCOVERY 1

a Kapan, setiap, **b** akan, **c** makan malam, makan malam, **d** Berapa

PRACTICE

1 a Kapan Anda/kamu makan pagi? **b** Saya akan berbelanja hari ini. **c** Saya tidur di hotel pada Rabu malam. **d** Setiap hari Minggu saya belajar bahasa Indonesia dan memasak makan malam.
2 a Linda will wake up tomorrow morning. **b** He will go to the mosque every Friday. **c** I will do homework tonight.
3 a Pak Frans memasak? **b** Jon makan siang di rumah setiap hari. **c** Ying makan pagi pada akhir minggu. **d** Budi memasak makan malam setiap malam.
4 Model answers:
Berapa umur Anda? Umur saya empat puluh satu tahun.
Berapa umur ibu Anda? Ibu saya berumur enam puluh tujuh tahun.
Berapa umur adik Anda? Umur adik saya sembilan belas tahun.

SPEAKING

1 Model answers:
Nani mandi dan pergi ke kantor pada hari Senin. Dia pulang dan memasak makan malam pada hari Selasa. Pada hari Rabu dia makan siang di kantor. Pada hari Kamis dia pergi ke bank dan tidur. Pada hari Jum'at dia makan siang di rumah orang tua dia. Nani menonton televisi dan mandi pada hari Sabtu. Dia belajar bahasa Inggris pada hari Minggu.

CONVERSATION 2

1 She is an engineer.
2 a at a foreign company. **b** twenty-eight years old. **c** She has to go to sleep. **d** Sleep well *or* Have a good sleep

3 a 2 a company, **b 1** an employee, **c 4** an engineer, **d 3** a helper

LANGUAGE DISCOVERY 2

a I work at a foreign company. **b** I am an engineer.

PRACTICE

1 a ekor, **b** buah, **c** orang, **d** buah

2 Model answers:

Apa pekerjaan Anda? Saya seorang pegawai di perusahaan Telindo. Dan Anda? Saya seorang akuntan, Apa pekerjaan kamu? Aku manajer di hotel. Dan kamu?

LISTENING

1 Monday – **7** woke up and ate breakfast at home, Tuesday – **1** went to the bank, Wednesday – **4** ate lunch at the office, Thursday – **5** called Jon, Friday – **3** went to the mosque, Saturday – **2** cooked in the kitchen, Sunday – **6** helped the children do their homework

2 Model answers:

a Hari ini hari Senin. **b** Saya mendengarkan radio pada hari Rabu. **c** Saya seorang pegawai negeri.

READING AND WRITING

2 Model answer:

Halo teman-teman! Saya Maria. Saya berumur enam puluh enam tahun. Saya seorang pensiunan. Saya senang membaca buku dan belajar bahasa Indonesia setiap hari. Pada akhir minggu, saya pergi ke gereja dengan anak tiri saya dan pasangan dia. Kami makan siang juga. Baiklah, saya akan menonton televisi sekarang. Selamat malam!

GO FURTHER

1 a 3 meneliti, research, **b 4** belajar, study, **c 1** melukis, paint, **d 2** menari, dance

2 Model answers:

a Dia seorang ilmuwan. **b** Dia seorang perawat.

TEST YOURSELF

1 a Kapan, **b** setiap Selasa malam, **c** pada akhir minggu, **d** pada hari Senin

2 a I shall help mother shop on Saturday. **b** They will cook tomorrow night. **c** I will go to church on Sunday.

3 a memasak makan pagi, **b** makan siang, **c** makan malam

4 a 2 He is fifteen years old. **b 3** She is thirty years old. **c 1** He is seventy years old.

5 a delapan orang anak, **b** sembilan belas orang pegawai negeri, **c** dua puluh lima buah televisi, **d** seorang pekerja LSM

6 a pekerjaan, **b** bekerja, **c** pelajar

Unit 5

SHOPPING

toko batik

VOCABULARY BUILDER

Shopping

credit card, discount

CONVERSATION 1

1 two hundred thousand rupiah

2 a Cobalah. **b** Tolong tunggu sebentar. **c** Silakan bayar di kasir.

3 a black, **b** 41, **c** he has to pay in cash

LANGUAGE DISCOVERY 1

a yang itu, yang biru, **b** Tolong, Silakan, **c** sepatu yang lebih murah, **d** ukuranmu, Ukuranku **e** harganya

PRACTICE

1 a Yang mana yang lebih murah? **b** Saya ambil yang itu. **c** Coba jas ini.

2 a Tolong, **b** Silakan

3 a Those shorts are too large. **b** These socks are not long enough.
c Thank you! The size is accurate.

4 a Aku tidak tahu ukuranku. **b** Ukuran kemejaku empat belas. **c** Roknya coklat dan rokmu abu-abu.

5 Model answers:

Berapa harga ponsel Anda? Harga ponsel saya tiga juta rupiah., Berapa harga kaos kakimu? Harganya seratus ribu rupiah., Berapa harga pasta gigimu? Harga pasta gigiku empat puluh lima ribu rupiah.

SPEAKING

Model answers:

a Saya berbelanja di pusat perbelanjaan. **b** Tidak. Kalau di Indonesia, saya tidak berbelanja di ruko. Saya berbelanja di mal. **c** Ukuranku tiga puluh enam.

CONVERSATION 2

1 a toothbrush
2 a 2 the dark blue one, **b 4** a twenty-thousand rupiah note, **c 1** ten thousand exactly, **d 3** change
4 a (light) green and (dark) blue, **b** toothpaste, **c** twenty thousand rupiah, **d** yes
5 Saya suka warna hijau dan warna biru tua., Saya ambil yang biru tua. Berapa harganya?, Tidak. Terima kasih. Saya tidak mau beli pasta gigi hari ini.

LANGUAGE DISCOVERY 2

a mau beli, **b** ada, Ada, **c** hijau muda, biru tua

PRACTICE

1 a boleh lihat, yang kuning, **b** mau pergi, warung
2 a Sorry. I don't have exact change. **b** Those sandals are still available, sir, and there is a 20 per cent discount!
3 Model answers:
Sendal saya putih. Kaos saya abu-abu. Celana pendek saya coklat tua., Ponsel saya kuning. Komputer saya hitam. Jas saya coklat muda.

LISTENING

1 a It is large. **b** It is being sold cheaply. **c** Three hundred million rupiah.
2 biru, enam setengah, Tidak ada, pasar swalayan, dijual, pasar swalayan, toserba

READING AND WRITING

1 Ira's

GO FURTHER

1 a sembilan ratus lima puluh rupiah, **b** empat ribu dua ratus rupiah, **c** dua belas ribu sembilan ratus rupiah, **d** tujuh ratus lima puluh ribu rupiah, **e** satu juta enam ratus dua puluh lima ribu rupiah
2 a 5 pharmacy, **b 1** electronics store, **c 4** arts and crafts market, **d 2** copy store, **e 3** bookstore
3 Model answers:
a Saya mau membeli oleh-oleh di pasar seni. **b** Saya paling suka warna abu-abu. **c** Harga belanjaan sehari-hari saya lima puluh ribu rupiah. **d** Di kota saya, aspirin dijual di apotek.

TEST YOURSELF

1 a Yang mana, **b** yang itu, **c** yang ini
2 a Tolong, **b** Silakan
3 a 2 not cheap enough, **b 3** smallest, **c 1** too large
4 a This is not my size. **b** Your size is seven and a half. **c** Its/her/his size is too small.
5 a Berapa harga rok pendek yang coklat? / Berapa harga rok coklat yang pendek? **b** Harganya tidak terlalu mahal.
6 a mau pergi, **b** boleh coba
7 a Tidak ada baju dalam di toko ini. **b** Kami ada kain-kain tradisional.
8 a pink, **b** dark green

Unit 6

ACCOMMODATION

saya perlu fasilitas air panas

VOCABULARY BUILDER

double, per night, confirmation

CONVERSATION 1

1 from May 30 to June 2
2 a Bisa saya bantu? **b** Tidak ada. **c** Berapa tarif kamar per malam?
3 a her husband, **b** double bed with a bathtub and no shower, **c** 130,000 rupiah per night

LANGUAGE DISCOVERY 1

a lebih suka, daripada, **b** kurang, **c** tanggal berapa, tanggal tiga puluh Mei

PRACTICE

1 a Mereka lebih suka losmen daripada hotel berbintang. **b** Saya lebih suka kamar mandi dengan fasilitas air panas. **c** Dia lebih suka menyewa kamar kos.
2 a Sorry. I don't quite like this room. **b** Guests do not like that hotel.
c They don't quite like living at a boarding house.
3 Model answers:
Hari ini tanggal berapa? Hari ini tanggal 27 September.
Tanggal berapa hari ini? Tanggal 4 Januari.

SPEAKING

Model answers:

Di kota Bandung, saya mau menginap di Losmen Tugu. Saya mau menginap dari tanggal tiga Februari sampai tanggal sepuluh Februari. Saya perlu dua kamar. Untuk tiga orang tamu.

Di Desa Mendut, saya mau menginap di Hotel Mataram. Saya mau menginap dari tanggal sembilan belas Februari sampai tanggal dua puluh lima Februari. Saya perlu satu kamar. Untuk dua orang tamu.

CONVERSATION 2

1 She has reserved a double room with air conditioning, an en-suite bathroom, and internet facilities from May 30 to June 2.
2 a 3 Betul. **b 1** Alamatnya Jalan Lumumba. **c 4** Kembali. **d 2** Belum.
4 a spell her name, **b** no, **c** Jalan Lumumba No. 35 *or* 35 Lumumba Street
5 Alamatnya Jalan Lumumba nomor tiga puluh lima., Bisa. L—U—M—U—M—B—A.

LANGUAGE DISCOVERY 2

1 a 2 the address, **b 1** the street name
2 a Di mana alamatnya? **b** Alamatnya Jalan Lumumba nomor tiga puluh lima.

PRACTICE

1 a Di mana kamar mandinya? **b** Siapa tamu barunya? **c** Di mana alamatnya?
2 Model answers:
Di mana alamatmu? Alamatku Jalan Queen Anne No. 20.
Di mana alamatnya? Alamatnya Jalan Asia-Afrika No. 6A.

LISTENING

1 a from July 6 to July 8, **b** 2 nights, **c** 40 dollars, **d** breakfast
2 Surabaya 03 Juni, Ambon 15 Januari, Manado 08 September, Semarang 17 April, Medan 11 Agustus, Batam 26 Februari, Padang 22 Juli, Jakarta 09 Maret, Makassar 24 Nopember

READING AND WRITING

2 a Taraji, **b** Tanggal, **c** JL. Kintamani No. 14, **d** Depok, **e** 16424, **f** (021)650-0592

GO FURTHER

1 a 6 non-smoking room, **b 3** extra bed, **c 8** cot, **d 7** safe, **e 2** iron and ironing board, **f 1** work desk, **g 9** tea and coffee maker, **h 5** hair dryer, **i 4** disability-friendly room

2 Apa arti 'internet gratis' dalam bahasa Inggris? Artinya 'free internet'. Apa arti 'unlimited wifi' dalam bahasa Indonesia? Artinya 'koneksi wifi tanpa batas'.
3 Model answers:
Di Indonesia, saya menginap di hotel berbintang dan di losmen.
Saya perlu tempat tidur ekstra, brankas, dan kamar bebas rokok.
Keperluan anak saya kolam renang. Keperluan-keperluan orang tua saya pancuran air mandi dan pembuat teh dan kopi.
Ya. Saya akan mencari kamar kos di Indonesia.

TEST YOURSELF

1 a Dia lebih suka kamar tanpa AC. **b** Budi lebih suka menginap di hotel berbintang. **c** Mereka lebih suka kamar dobel daripada kamar singel.
2 a Saya kurang suka menginap di penginapan. **b** Aku kurang suka menyewa kamar kos. **c** Mereka kurang suka menelpon pada akhir minggu.
3 a tanggal berapa, **b** pada tanggal 17 Januari, **c** tanggal 23 September.
4 a Where is the hotel? **b** How much is the room rate per night? **c** What is the office phone number? **d** For how many guests?
5 a Di mana, **b** kepada, **c** Jalan, **d** Apa

R2

1 a 3 Thursday, **b 8** Sunday, **c 4** day, **d 9** Friday, **e 6** Wednesday, **f 1** Monday, **g 5** Saturday, **h 10** month, **i 7** week, **j 2** year
2 a Berapa umur kamu? *or* Umur kamu berapa? **b** Kapan mereka mandi? **c** Kamu cari apa? **d** Kamu mau beli apa? **e** Berapa ukuranmu? *or* Ukuranmu berapa? **f** Berapa harganya? *or* Harganya berapa? **g** Yang mana? **h** Di mana kamu menginap? *or* Kamu menginap di mana? **i** Di mana alamatnya? *or* Alamatnya di mana? **j** Ada fasilitas internet?
3 a Selamat tidur. **b** Silakan bayar di kasir. **c** Tolong tunggu sebentar. **d** Belilah. **e** Hari ini hari Selasa, tanggal tujuh belas Agustus. **f** Maaf. **g** Yang paling murah.
4 went to the office – pergi ke kantor, having breakfast – makan pagi, this week – minggu ini, busy – sibuk, will wake up – akan bangun, look for – cari, department store – toserba, souvenirs – oleh-oleh, arts and crafts market – pasar seni, the prices – harga-harganya, many – banyak, at the weekend – pada akhir minggu
5 a seventeen years, **b** an engineer, **c** nine months, **d** ten people, **e** (the year) one thousand seven hundred (and) sixty-two, **f** one million five hundred thousand rupiah

6 a Anisa's father, **b** dark brown, **c** to wear them to the office, **d** one hundred thousand rupiah, **e** a new cellphone battery and a pair of yellow sandals, **f** they were not available at the mall
7 a pasang, **b** ekor, **c** orang, **d** buah
8 a Carilah losmen. **b** Tolong bantu saya. **c** Silakan menginap di rumah kami.
9 a 3 Tidak apa-apa. **b 6** Terima kasih kembali. **c 5** Yang ini lebih murah. **d 2** Sampai nanti! **e 4** Artinya *'contactless'*. **f 1** Maaf. Yang ini tidak dijual.
10 a Berapa tarif kamar per malam pada bulan Maret? **b** Saya mau memesan kamar dobel. **c** Anda sudah ada reservasi di hotel kami?
11 a a foreign company, **b** homemaker, **c** the goods there are the cheapest ones, **d** every Friday, **e** small, **f** an Australian student, **g** in November
12 internet access, air conditioning, en-suite bathroom, hot water, shower
13 Tono, at the till there is no change. I don't have exact change. Do you have a fifty-thousand-rupiah note?
14 a Ningsih Suparman, **b** 12 Juli 1980, **c** pekerja LSM, **d** Jalan Sadikin No. 34, **e** Jakarta, **f** 101622, **g** 0215365701
15 a three months, **b** three bedrooms, two bathrooms, **c** a small kitchen, **d** a large porch and a swimming pool, **e** they can pay it in dollars or rupiah

Unit 7

TRANSPORTATION

ongkos perjalanan

VOCABULARY BUILDER

Traveling
return, one-way

Time
minute

CONVERSATION 1

1 his passport
2 a naik kelas ekonomi, **b** Saya belum tahu. **c** Selamat tinggal.
3 a 3.45 p.m., **b** an open-date return ticket, **c** one suitcase

LANGUAGE DISCOVERY 1

a naik kelas ekonomi, **b** pada jam empat kurang seperempat sore

PRACTICE

1 a Jon takes a plane to Padang. **b** Ita rode a motorcycle to her mother's house. **c** Dimas is traveling by underground train to the office.
2 a jam sebelas lewat lima belas (*or* lewat seperempat) siang, **b** jam sembilan kurang sepuluh menit pagi, **c** jam setengah tujuh malam
3 Model answers:
Kereta api berangkat pada jam dua belas lewat seperempat siang.
Ferinya akan sampai di Lombok pada jam sepuluh kurang sepuluh pagi.
Saya mau memesan taksi untuk jam setengah delapan malam.

SPEAKING

1 Model answer:
Helen pergi ke kantor naik mobil pada jam tujuh pagi. Dia pergi makan siang naik bus pada jam dua belas siang. Dia kembali ke kantor naik ojek pada jam setengah dua siang. Dia pulang ke rumah naik mobil pada jam lima lewat dua puluh sore.
2 Model answer:
Saya pergi ke universitas naik kereta bawah tanah pada jam sepuluh pagi. Saya pergi makan siang naik taksi pada jam satu siang. Saya pulang ke rumah naik bus pada jam setengah sembilan malam.

CONVERSATION 2

1 twenty-five minutes
2 a 3 I'm going to Solo. **b 1** What time is it now? **c 2** What time is the bus leaving?
4 a the bus to Semarang, **b** at 1.15 p.m., **c** on the bus or at the ticket booth
5 Ibu bisa naik bus jurusan Semarang di sini., Busnya berangkat pada jam satu lewat seperempat siang., Jam satu kurang sepuluh.

LANGUAGE DISCOVERY 2

a Loketnya di situ. **b** Bus itu baru berangkat. **c** Mau ke mana, Bu?

PRACTICE

1 a Bus Anda/kamu akan berhenti di situ. **b** Anda/Kamu bisa beli tiket bus Anda/kamu di sini. **c** Jon berangkat dari sana pada jam setengah lima sore.
2 a The airplane from Ambon just/recently arrived. **b** He just/recently bought a plane ticket. **c** They just paid the trip fare.
3 Model answers:
Anda mau pergi ke mana? Saya mau pergi ke hotel saya.
Mau ke mana? Mau ke kantor.

LISTENING

1 a 7 a.m. and 8 a.m., **b** two hours, **c** ninety thousand rupiah

2 a traveling to Trawas – **5** by car, **b** going to Madura – **4** by ship, **c** going into the city – **1** by taxi, **d** getting to the market – **3** go on foot, **e** when you have no time – **2** by motorcycle service

3 Model answers:

Sekarang jam setengah lima sore., Saya berangkat dari rumah pada jam tujuh pagi., Saya sampai di kantor kira-kira pada jam setengah sembilan pagi.

READING AND WRITING

2 Model answer:

YTh. Tante Agatha,

Aku datang ke Indonesia pada bulan September. Sebelum belajar di sekolah bahasa, aku naik pesawat terbang dari Denpasar ke Surabaya. Tiketnya tidak mahal. Dari Surabaya, aku naik mobil ke Blitar. Banyak orang naik sepeda motor di kota itu. Aku kembali ke Bali naik feri. Di Bali, aku jalan kaki dari rumah kos ke sekolah bahasa. Aku senang di sini.

GO FURTHER

1 a morning, **b** 10, 3, **c** afternoon, **d** evening

2 a Saya sampai (*or* datang) di Indonesia pada malam hari. **b** Saya berangkat pada pagi hari. **c** Saya akan naik kereta bawah tanah pada siang hari. **d** Dia akan datang ke Lembang naik kereta api pada sore hari.

3 Model answers:

a Di Jakarta, sekarang pukul sembilan malam WIB., Di London, sekarang pukul dua siang GMT.

b Saya datang dari rumah saya., Saya datang dari Inggris.

c Ya. Aku mau datang ke rumahmu., Tidak. Aku tidak mau.

d Terima kasih. Aku sampai pada pagi hari., Terima kasih! Aku sampai pada jam dua siang.

TEST YOURSELF

1 pesawat terbang, tiket sekali jalan, Perjalanan, (pergi) naik mobil, naik taksi, naik ojek, naik, jurusan, turun

2 a 3.40 p.m. *or* twenty to four in the afternoon, **b** 9.15 a.m. *or* a quarter past nine in the morning, **c** 7.30 p.m. *or* half past seven in the evening, **d** 12 p.m. *or* twelve noon

3 a Pada jam berapa bus jurusan Madiun datang? **b** Mobil mereka sampai pada jam sebelas malam. **c** Jam berapa Anda mau berangkat? **d** Jam berapa kereta berikutnya berangkat?

4 a sini, **b** sana, **c** situ
5 a Kapal baru berangkat. **b** Penumpang-penumpang baru turun feri.
6 b Mau di mana?

Unit 8

CUISINE

seporsi (*or* satu porsi) nasi

VOCABULARY BUILDER

Cooking methods

1 a goreng – **4** to fry *or* fried, **b** rebus – **1** to boil *or* boiled, **c** bakar/panggang – **2** to roast/grill *or* roasted/grilled, **d** kukus – **5** to steam *or* steamed, **e** tumis – **3** to stir-fry *or* stir-fried

Popular menu items

prawn cracker, meat skewer, curry, soup

CONVERSATION 1

1 sweet iced tea, hot tea, iced coffee, cold water without ice
2 a Yang mana yang enak? **b** Dan ini makanan Anda datang sekarang.
c Tolong ambilkan saya satu sedotan.
3 a one bowl of egg noodle soup, one glass of iced coffee, and two portions of chicken skewers, **b** a straw, **c** Enjoy your meal

LANGUAGE DISCOVERY 1

a memesan, **b** pesanan, **c** secangkir, **d** yang pedas, pedas

PRACTICE

1 a rebus, boil, **b** goreng, fry, **c** kukus, steam
2 a makanan, food, **b** minuman, drink, **c** masakan, cooking *or* cuisine
3 a Grandfather wishes to order a cup of unsweetened/black coffee.
b My younger sister does not want a bowl of chicken soup. **c** They want a portion of soy grilled fish.
4 Model answers:
Saya suka yang tidak pahit. Yang mana tidak pahit?, Saya suka yang asin. Yang mana asin?, Saya suka yang tidak pedas. Yang mana tidak pedas?

SPEAKING

Model answers:

Saya mau meja untuk satu orang.

Saya ingin memesan sepiring nasi goreng ikan asin yang pedas, satu porsi tahu dan tempe, dua potong kue bolu kukus, secangkir kopi luwak manis, dan segelas jus alpukat.

CONVERSATION 2

1 the grilled (*or* roasted) fish

2 a enak sekali, **b** masih lapar, **c** sudah selesai, **d** makan bersama

4 a eatery *or* restaurant, **b** the server did not hear him, **c** to clear the table, **d** on Saturday

5 Maaf. Jum'at ini saya akan makan bersama Yati., Sabtu? Bisa. Aku bisa makan bersama kamu pada hari Sabtu.

LANGUAGE DISCOVERY 2

a sepiring *or* satu piring kare lagi, **b** ambilkan bonnya, **c** bersama

PRACTICE

1 a Father wants another (*or* one more) plate of chicken rice. **b** Three more portions of goat skewers, please.

2 a Tolong ambilkan bon kami. **b** Tolong minta bonnya.

3 Model answers:

Mari makan., Anda mau makan siang bersama saya?, Kamu mau makan bersama?

LISTENING

1 a to be taken away, **b** iced coconut water, **c** rice, fried shrimp, and two fried soy bean cakes

2 Model answers:

Saya ingin memesan makanan untuk dibawa pulang. Saya mau satu porsi ayam lada hitam, satu sop tahu, satu porsi lontong, dan satu kepiting asam manis.

Saya mau satu nasi, satu mie, dan dua porsi udang bakar. Tolong dibungkus, ya?

READING AND WRITING

2 Saya tidak bisa makan bersama kalian siang ini tetapi di meja makan ada makanan dan minuman yang enak untuk kalian semua. Ada lontong, nasi, sate kambing, udang rebus, air jeruk, dan jus alpukat. Selamat makan!

GO FURTHER

1 a sumpit – **3** chopsticks, **b** sendok teh – **5** teaspoon, **c** pisau – **1** knife, **d** pisau dapur – **2** kitchen knife, **e** sendok garpu – **4** cutlery

2 a soy sauce, **b** sweet soy sauce, **c** chili sauce

3 Model answers:

a Ya. Saya perlu sendok garpu. Ya. saya perlu sebuah pisau dan sepasang sumpit. **b** Boleh. Saya boleh minum minuman beralkohol. Tidak. Saya tidak boleh minum alkohol. **c** Ya. Saya punya alergi kacang tanah. Tidak. Saya tidak beralergi.

TEST YOURSELF

1 a We will wait for our food. **b** Mr Bejo is wrapping (*or* repackaging) their drinks. **c** She/He is taking home Yati's cooking. **d** I wish to change my order.

2 a Bubur sagu makanan dari Maluku. **b** Babi panggang masakan tradisional di Toba. **c** Air jeruk hangat minuman sehat.

3 a Saya ingin memesan segelas (*or* satu gelas) air dingin dan dua gelas bir. **b** Istrinya mau makan seporsi (*or* satu porsi) lontong. **c** Anak-anak saya mau satu ikan bakar dan dua mie goreng daging sapi. **d** Mereka mau empat cangkir teh tawar.

4 a Yang mana tidak asin? **b** Kalau Anda suka yang manis, cobalah singkong goreng. **c** Mereka ingin coba susu kedelai kami? **d** Saya tidak makan daging.

5 a satu kopi lagi, **b** dua porsi nasi lagi

6 a 3 How much is it all? **b 1** Please fetch the check. **c 2** May I ask for the check?

7 a bersama, **b** bersama, **c** Mari, **d** Siapa, memesan/pesan bersama

Unit 9

FINDING YOUR WAY

Saya perlu bantuan

VOCABULARY BUILDER

Places

a kantor pos – **5** post office, **b** kantor polisi – **6** police station, **c** stasiun kereta – **7** train station, **d** halte bus – **10** bus stop, **e** bandara – **9** airport, **f** kedutaan – **3** embassy, **g** warnet – **11** internet café, **h** bioskop – **2** cinema, **i** tempat parkir – **8** parking space/car park, **j** tempat penyeberangan – **1** crossing/crosswalk, **k** WC umum – **4** public restroom

CONVERSATION 1

1 to the British embassy
2 a dekat (near) - **2** jauh (far), **b** pertama (first) - **4** terakhir (last), **c** kiri (left) - **1** kanan (right), **d** betul (correct) - **3** salah (incorrect)
3 a a map, **b** police station and post office, **c** Jalan (*or* Street) Adipati, **d** a Catholic church (Santa Maria *or* St. Mary's)

LANGUAGE DISCOVERY 1

a Bagaimana caranya, **b** kedua, **c** di seberang

PRACTICE

1 a Bagaimana caranya pergi ke stasiun kereta? **b** Bagaimana caranya ke tempat parkir? **c** Bagaimana caranya jalan kaki ke bank dari sini?
2 a 2 first, **b 3** sixth, **c 1** fourth
3 Model answer:
Bank di sebelah kanan toko buku. Kantor pos di antara apotek dan restoran Nusa Dua. Halte bus di depan gereja. Warnet di belakang bioskop. Kantor polisi di seberang jalan dari bioskop. Apartemen saya di atas supermarket. Tempat parkir di bawah Hotel Lido.

SPEAKING

Model answer:
Halte bus yang paling dekat di depan kantor saya.
Model answer:
Pertama, keluar rumahku dan belok kiri. Jalan terus sampai Jalan Flask. Kemudian belok kanan di persimpangan itu dan jalan kaki sampai stasiun kereta Hampstead. Naik kereta bawah tanah sampai stasiun Euston. Turun di situ, lalu ganti kereta. Naik kereta jurusan Victoria sampai stasiun Charing Cross. Turun di sana dan keluar stasiun. Terakhir, belok kiri.

CONVERSATION 2

1 the internet café
2 a Bagaimana caranya pergi ke sana? **b** Aku kurang tahu di mana itu. **c** Tidak usah, terima kasih. **d** Mari ikut saya.
4 a on the third floor, in front of the internet café, **b** Linda can take the escalator, elevator/lift, or stairs, **c** Eva offers to escort her there, **d** Eva needs to go upstairs
5 Tidak usah, terima kasih. Aku akan cari sendiri., Terima kasih. Maaf, aku merepotkan kamu.

LANGUAGE DISCOVERY 2

a lantai tiga, **b** Saya, sendiri, **c** Tidak usah

PRACTICE

1 a lantai satu, **b** lantai dua

2 a I eat by myself **b** I will go home on my own.

3 Model answers:

Tidak usah, terima kasih. Saya akan cari sendiri., Terima kasih. Maaf, saya merepotkan Anda.

LISTENING

1 a It is forbidden to park where he is going. **b** The sidewalk is slippery. **c** He does not need to walk quickly.

2 a kantor polisi, **b** apotek, **c** kantor pos, **d** alun-alun, **e** rumah makan, **f** warnet, **g** apartemen

READING AND WRITING

1 a 3 dilarang parkir 08:00–18:00, **b 1** awas jalan licin, **c 4** dilarang menyeberang, **d 2** dilarang berhenti di sini

2 Model answer:

Teman-teman, turun bus di halte bus di depan apotek. Belok kiri dan masuk Jalan Gunawarman. Jalan lurus terus sampai persimpangan jalan itu dan Jalan Rusa. Belok kanan. Restorannya di seberang jalan dari bank.

GO FURTHER

1 a lantai atas – **3** upper floor, **b** lantai bawah – **5** lower floor, **c** pertigaan – **4** T-junction, **d** perempatan – **2** intersection *or* crossroads, **e** bundaran – **1** roundabout

2 a I go down the escalator slowly. **b** You cross quickly. **c** Mrs Dewi parks carefully. **d** Please repeat slowly.

3 Model answers:

Caranya mengeja nama saya begini, W—A—N—T—A—G—E.

Caranya begini, dari rumah saya, pergi ke stasiun kereta bawah tanah. Kemudian naik kereta bawah tanah ke Stasiun Paddington dan ganti kereta di sana. Naik kereta jurusan Heathrow dan turun di bandara Heathrow.

TEST YOURSELF

1 Bagaimana caranya, Belok, terus, lampu merah, belok kanan, persimpangan *or* perempatan, menyeberang

2 a halte pertama, **b** orang terakhir, **c** anak kedua

3 a 3 side, **b 5** between, **c 1** behind, **d 6** outside, **e 4** in front of, **f 2** across
4 a bawah, **b** dua, **c** atas, **d** berapa
5 a I don't live by myself. **b** Anisa works by herself in her house. **c** They walked about on their own in Tebing Tinggi. **d** Will Rosa go on her own or with you to the airport?
6 a Mari, saya antar Anda. **b** Tidak usah, terima kasih. **c** Tolong/Silakan, Bu, ikut saya. **d** Maaf, saya merepotkan Anda.

Unit 10

HEALTH

praktik – practice, pasien – patient

VOCABULARY BUILDER

Health
kepala – head, perut – stomach, tenggorokan – throat, kulit – skin, gigi – teeth, dokter anak – pediatrician

Medical procedures
operasi – operation

CONVERSATION 1
1 she has a headache and her neck hurts
2 a Ada apa, Bu? **b** Karena saya mau minta janji dengan dia.
c Sebaiknya Ibu diperiksa hari ini.
3 a no, **b** three days, **c** she will need to have an x-ray taken

LANGUAGE DISCOVERY 1
a sakit kepala, sakit, diperiksa oleh, **b** ada, berada, **c** minggu lalu, yang lalu, **d** Sesudah, **e** Sejak

PRACTICE

1 a My back hurts/aches. **b** My leg/foot and knee are wounded.
2 a Maaf, Bu Dokter tidak ada. Saya berbicara dengan siapa? **b** Kapan Anda berada di Indonesia?
3 a Seorang penari dironsen lima bulan yang lalu. **b** Anda/Kamu akan dioperasi minggu depan.
4 a after, **b** before
5 Model answers:
a Sejak empat bulan yang lalu. **b** Mulai dari hari Senin saya berlibur.

SPEAKING

Model answers:

Saya mau minta janji dengan dokter anak., Untuk hari Rabu. Saya bisa datang pada jam setengah lima sore.

CONVERSATION 2

1 He tells Jon not to eat carelessly after this.
2 a minum obat ini, **b** resep obat antibiotik, **c** membeli obatnya, **d** menebus resepnya
4 a since two days ago, **b** stomach ache, vomiting, going to the toilet often, **c** he sometimes eats carelessly and he often forgets to eat, **d** at the pharmacy
5 Saya sering harus pergi ke WC., Tidak selalu. Saya kadang-kadang makan sembarangan. Dan saya sering lupa makan.

LANGUAGE DISCOVERY 2

a tiga kali sehari, **b** jangan, **c** sering lupa makan

PRACTICE

1 a Saya praktik di rumah sakit empat kali seminggu. **b** Kulit saya diperiksa sekali/satu kali setahun.
2 a Tolong jangan lupa janji Anda dengan dokter!, **b** Jangan makan sebelum Anda dioperasi.
3 Model answers:
a Tidak. Saya tidak sering berlibur. Saya jarang berlibur.
b Saya biasanya makan di warung.

LISTENING

1 a she rode a motorcycle carelessly, **b** on her face and nose but she didn't need an x-ray, **c** two weeks from now
2 a 2 hip bone fracture, **b 3** influenza, **c 1** toothache
Model answer:
Semoga cepat sembuh, Siti!, Semoga cepat sembuh!, Semoga cepat sembuh, Ibu Tuti!

READING AND WRITING

2 Model answer: Zadie, apa kabar? Aku dengar sejak minggu lalu kamu tidak enak badan. Apakah kamu sudah merasa lebih baik hari ini? Semoga cepat sembuh! Salam hangat, Maggie.

GO FURTHER

1 a I never study. **b** I have studied Indonesian (language) before.
2 Model answers:
a Sampai bulan depan., Sampai saya selesai. **b** Ya. Saya kadang-kadang perlu kursi roda., Tidak. Saya tidak pernah perlu kursi roda. **c** Sudah. Saya sudah pernah berlibur di Indonesia., Belum. Saya belum pernah berlibur di Indonesia.

TEST YOURSELF

1 sakit perut – had a stomach ache, minta janji dengan – requested an appointment with, diperiksa – was examined, resep obat – prescription, minum obat itu – took that medicine, merasa – felt, Sejak – Since
2 a Maaf, ada apa, Pak Jon? **b** Perawat-perawat berada di puskesmas. **c** Bu Dokter ada? **d** Siapa berada di kamar tunggu?
3 a 2 two weeks ago, **b 3** next week, **c 1** two weeks from now
4 a Please take the medicine after dinner. **b** The day after tomorrow you will be x-rayed before being examined by the doctor. **c** My ankle hurt before I was operated on.
5 a until, **b** since
6 a Berapa kali seminggu? **b** Minum obat in tiga kali sehari. *or* Minum obat ini sehari tiga kali. **c** Perawat datang sekali setiap jam. *or* Perawat datang setiap jam sekali.
7 a Jangan, **b** Jangan, **c** Tolong, jangan
8 a sering berlibur, **b** tidak sering, **c** tidak pernah diperiksa, **d** selalu sakit

R3

1 a Jam berapa sekarang? *or* Sekarang jam berapa? **b** Yang mana kereta yang paling cepat? *or* Kereta yang paling cepat yang mana? **c** Ada meja untuk enam orang? **d** Selamat makan. **e** Tolong bonnya. **f** Numpang tanya ..., **g** Bagaimana cara naik bus ke pasar swalayan (*or* supermarket)? **h** Tolong ulang pelan-pelan, **i** Maaf, saya/aku merepotkan Anda/kamu. **j** Jangan lupa.
2 a 3 Tiga puluh ribu rupiah. **b 5** Enam jam. **c 1** Selamat tinggal. **d 6** Terima kasih. **e 4** Tidak usah. **f 2** Tidak ada apa-apa.
3 a cold, **b** 4:30 p.m., two hours, **c** the motorcycle service was not available, the taxi was available, **d** her family's house, the food was still warm and the soup was very delicious, **e** next week, **f** playing with her nieces and nephews

4 a 3 no parking, **b 5** no crossing, **c 2** beware of slippery sidewalk, **d 1** do not stop here, **e 4** do not walk here

5 a 6:45 a.m., **b** 3:10 p.m., **c** a bowl of chicken rice porridge that is not spicy, **d** a glass of iced coffee, **e** two bottles of mineral water, **f** the eighth patient

6 a four portions/orders of goat skewers, two portions/orders of steamed rice cake, two portions/orders of spicy egg fried rice, because her family is hungry, **b** spicy food, **c** spicy noodle soup, black pepper roasted/grilled chicken, she says the chicken is delicious, **d** another sweetened iced soy milk, **e** satu es susu kedelai tidak manis, satu es susu kedelai tanpa gula, **f** she asks how much it costs and she tells him she will pay for it herself

7 a Saya beralergi kacang tanah. **b** Perawat mengantar saya ke kamar kecil. **c** Tolong ambilkan sendok garpu. **d** Saya suka kentang goreng yang tidak asin. *or* Saya tidak suka kentang goreng yang asin. **e** Hitomi mau minta janji dengan dokter umum.

8 a haus, **b** kecap, **c** lusa, **d** lalu, **e** tahu, **f** asam

9 tidak jauh – not far, pasar – market, dekat – near, tempat penyeberangan – crosswalk, lampu merah – traffic light, di seberang jalan dari – across the street from, apotek di lantai tiga – pharmacy on the 3rd floor, di antara – between, di lantai atas – on the upper floor, di sebelah – next to, di belakang – behind

10 a makan, **b** periksa, **c** operasi, **d** rasa, **e** tekan, **f** antar

11 a Sejak, **b** Sampai, **c** dari, **d** kali, **e** Kalian, **f** Ada

12 a Dear, **b** two months ago, **c** started, **d** a journalist, **e** always, **f** sometimes, **g** rarely, **h** why, **i** said, **j** because, **k** never, **l** felt unwell, **m** had the flu, **n** get well soon, **o** he took the medicine four times a day, **p** your son's/child's health, **q** contact, **r** three days from now, **s** Happy New Year

13 the way – caranya, first – pertama, get on – naik, ninety-nine – sembilan puluh sembilan, get off – turun, Enter – Masuk, roughly – kira-kira, If – Kalau, intersection – persimpangan *or* perempatan, there is – ada, Turn left – Belok kiri, keep walking straight – jalan lurus terus, after – sesudah, Finally – Terakhir, eighty-eight – delapan puluh delapan

Indonesian–English glossary

Here is a list of all the Indonesian vocabulary included in this book. The Indonesian words have been listed alphabetically. To get you started on how Indonesian dictionaries work, words that have also been presented in root form are only listed in root form unless there is a difference in meaning. For example, **bekerja** (*work*) is only listed as **kerja** (*to work*) but **ambil** (*to take*) and **ambilkan** (*to fetch*) are separate entries.

abu-abu	*gray*
ada	*there is/are, has/have, to be available, to be present (somewhere)*
Ada apa?	*What's the matter?*
Apa kabar?	*How are you?*
adik	*younger sibling*
Agustus	*August*
air	*water*
air jeruk	*citrus drink*
akan	*will, going to, shall*
akhir	*end* (n.)
akomodasi	*accommodation*
aku	*I, me, my*
akuntan	*accountant*
alamat	*address*
alergi	*allergy*
alkohol	*alcohol*
alpukat	*avocado*
alun-alun	*square* (loc.)
ambil	*take* (v.)
ambilkan	*to fetch*
ambulans	*ambulance*
Amerika	*America*
Amerika Serikat	*USA*
anak	*child*
anak angkat	*adopted child*
anak tiri	*stepchild*
Anda	*you, your*
angkat	*to lift (up)*
angklung	*bamboo musical instrument*
antar	*escort*
antara	*between*
antibiotik	*antibiotic*
antiseptik	*antiseptic*
apa	*what*
Apakah	(interrogative in yes/no questions)
apakah	*whether, if*
api	*fire*
apotek	*pharmacy*
April	*April*
Arab	*Arab*
arti	*meaning*
asal	*origin*
asam	*sour*
asin	*salty*
asing	*foreign*
atas	*above,* (coll.) *upstairs*
atau	*or*
Australia	*Australia*
awas	*beware (of)*
ayah	*father*

ayam	*chicken*
Ayo!	*Come!, Come on!*
babi	*pig*
badan	*body*
bagaimana	*how*
bagaimana kalau	*how would it be if,* (coll.) *what about*
bagasi	*luggage*
bagus	*good, well done*
bahasa	*language*
bahu	*shoulder*
baik	*good, well*
Baiklah.	*All right., Okay.*
baju	*clothing*
baju dalam	*underclothes*
bak mandi	*bathtub*
bakar	*to roast/grill*
bandar udara	*airport*
bandara	*airport*
bank	*bank*
bantu	*help* (v.), *assist* (v.)
bantuan	*help* (n.)
Bapak	*Sir, Mr*
bapak	*father*
barang	*thing, object, goods*
barat	*west*
baru	*new, recently, just, newly*
batas	*limit*
baterai	*battery*
bawa	*to carry, to take (away)*
bawah	*below,* (coll.) *downstairs*
bawah tanah	*underground*
bayam	*spinach*
bayar	*pay* (v.)
bayi	*baby*
bebas	*be free*
bebek	*duck* (n.)
begini	*like this*
begitu	*like that*
belajar	*study* (v.)
belakang	*back* (loc.)
belanja	*shop* (v.)
belanjaan	*shopping* (n.)
belas	*-teen*
beli	*buy*
beliau	*he/she, him/her, his/her* (formal)
belok	*to turn*
belum	*not yet*
beralergi	*to have an allergy*
beralkohol	*containing alcohol*
berangkat	*depart*
berapa	*how many*
berasal	*come from, originate*
berbintang	*star-rated*
berhenti	*stop* (v.)
berikut	*following, next*
berjalan-jalan	*walking about*
berkata	*say* (v.)
berkenalan	*to become acquainted*
berlatih	*train* (v.)
berlibur	*to be on vacation*
bermain	*play* (v.)
bermata	*to have ... eyes*
bersama	*together, (along) with*
berselam skuba	*scuba diving*
berselancar	*surfing*
bertemu	*meet* (v.)
bertetangga	*be/become neighbors*
berumur	*to be aged*
besar	*large*
besok	*tomorrow*
betul	*correct*
biasanya	*usually*
bibi	*aunt*
bibir	*lip, lips*
bicara	*speak, converse*
bidan	*midwife*
bilang	*say* (coll., v.)
bioskop	*cinema*
bir	*beer*
biru	*blue*
bis (coll.)	*bus* (n.)
bisa	*can, able to*
boleh	*may, to be allowed to*
bolu	*sponge (cake)*

bon	*check, bill*	desa	*village*
botol	*bottle*	Desember	*December*
brankas	*safe* (n.)	di	*at/in/on*
buah	*fruit* (thing classifier)	dia	*he/she, him/her, his/her*
buat	*do (something)*		
buatkan	*create (for)*	dibawa pulang	*to be taken home*
bubur	*porridge*	dibungkus	*to be wrapped*
bukan	*no, not*	diinfus	*to be put on an IV drip*
buku	*book*	dijual	*for sale, to be sold*
bulan	*month*	dilarang	*forbidden*
bulu tangkis	*badminton*	dingin	*cold*
bundaran	*roundabout*	dioperasi	*to be operated on*
bungkus	*to wrap*	dirawat	*be nursed, treated, cared for*
burung	*bird*		
bus	*bus* (n.)	dirawat jalan	*be cared for as an outpatient*
cangkir	*cup*		
cara	*method*	dirawat inap	*be cared for as an inpatient*
cari	*look for, search for*		
catur	*chess*	dironsen	*to be x-rayed*
celana	*pants*	diskon	*discount*
cepat	*quick, early*	dokter	*doctor*
cepat-cepat	*quickly*	dokter anak	*pediatrician*
cerita	*story*	dokter gigi	*dentist*
Cina	*China*	dokter umum	*general practitioner*
coba	*to try*	domba	*sheep*
cokelat	*brown*	dua	*two*
cucu	*grandchild*	duduk	*sit*
dada	*chest*	ekor	*tail* (animal classifier)
daging	*meat*	ekstra	*extra*
dah	*goodbye*	elektronik	*electronic*
dalam	*inside, within, in*	emas	*gold*
dan	*and*	empat	*four*
danau	*lake*	enak	*delicious*
dapur	*kitchen*	enam	*six*
dari	*from*	Eropa	*Europe*
daripada	*than*	es	*ice, iced*
dasi	*tie*	eskalator	*escalator*
datang	*come, arrive*	fasilitas	*amenity, facility*
dekat	*near*	Februari	*February*
delapan	*eight*	feri	*ferry*
dengan	*with*	film	*film*
dengar	*to hear*	flu	*flu, influenza*
depan	*front, ahead*	fotokopi	*photocopy*

gamelan	*Indonesian traditional percussion ensemble*	ikut	*follow*
gang	*alley*	ilmuwan	*scientist*
ganti	*switch* (v.), *change* (v.)	India	*India*
garam	*salt*	infus	*intravenous (IV) therapy*
gatal	*itch* (v., n.)	Inggris	*England*
gawai	*work* (n.)	ingin	*want, wish* (v.)
gayung	*(water) dipper*	ini	*this*
gelas	*glass*	insinyur	*engineer*
gemar	*enjoy, be pleased*	Irlandia	*Ireland*
gemuk	*plump*	istri	*wife*
gereja	*church*	itu	*that*
gigi	*tooth*	jadi	*so, thus, therefore*
goreng	*to fry*	jagung	*corn*
gratis	*free*	jahe	*ginger*
gunung	*mountain*	jalan	*street, road, way*
habis	*to be finished, to have run out*	jalan kaki	*walk, travel on foot*
halaman	*yard, garden, page*	jam	*hour, clock*
halo	*hello* (phone greeting)	jangan	*do not* (imperative)
halte bus	*bus stop*	janji	(coll.) *appointment*
hamil	*to be pregnant*	jantung	*heart*
hangat	*warm*	Januari	*January*
hanya	*only*	jarang	*rarely*
harga	*price*	jari	*finger*
hari	*day*	jari kaki	*toe*
harus	*must*	jas	*blazer, coat*
hati	*liver*, (fig.) *heart*	jatuh	*fall (down)*
hati-hati	*carefully, to be careful*	jauh	*far*
haus	*thirsty*	Jawa	*Java*
hidung	*nose*	jembatan	*bridge*
hidup	*life*	Jepang	*Japan*
hijau	*green*	jeruk	*citrus (orange, lime, etc.)*
hitam	*black*	jual	*sell*
hotel	*hotel*	juga	*too, also*
HP	*hand phone*	Juli	*July*
hubungi	*contact* (vt.)	Jum'at	*Friday*
ibu	*mother*	Juni	*June*
Ibu	*Madam, Mrs, Ms*	jurusan	*destination, heading (for)*
ibu jari	*thumb*	jus	*juice*
ibu rumah tangga	*homemaker*	juta	*million*
ikan	*fish*	kabar	*news*
iklan	*advert*	kacang	*nut, pea, bean*
		kacang tanah	*peanut*

kadang-kadang *sometimes*
kain *cloth*
kakak *older sibling*
kakek *grandfather*
kaki *leg*
kalau *if, when*
kali *(number of) times/ occasions*
kalian *you, your* (plural, informal)
kamar dobel *double room*
kamar kecil *toilet* (fig.)
kamar kos *bedsit*
kamar mandi *bathroom*
kamar singel *single room*
kambing *goat*
kami *we/us/our* (exclusive)
Kamis *Thursday*
kampung *village*
kamu *you, your*
Kanada *Canada*
kanan *right*
kanguru *kangaroo*
kantor *office*
kantor polisi *police station*
kantor pos *post office*
kaos *T-shirt*
kaos kaki *socks*
kapal *ship*
Kapan *When* (interrogative)
karcis *ticket*
kare *curry*
karena *because*
kartu *card*
karyawan *worker, employee*
Kasihan! *What a pity!, Poor thing!*
kasir *cashier, till* (coll.)
ke *to*
kecap *soy sauce*
kecelakaan *accident,* (coll.) *have an accident*
kecil *small*
kedelai *soy*
kedua *second*
kedutaan *embassy*
keju *cheese*
kelapa *coconut*
keluar *exit* (v.)
keluarga *family*
kemarin *yesterday*
kembali *return* (v.)
Kembali. *(Thanks) in return., You're welcome.*
kemeja *shirt*
kemudian *then*
kenal *recognize, know*
kenalan *acquaintance*
Kenalkan. *Let me introduce you.*
kenalkan *to acquaint (someone)*
kenapa *why*
kendaraan *vehicle*
kendaraan umum *public transport*
kentang *potato*
kenyang *full* (as in *sated)*
kepada *to (someone)*
kepala *head*
kepiting *crab*
keponakan *niece, nephew*
kepulauan *archipelago*
kereta api *train* (n.)
kerja *to work*
kesehatan *health*
ketiga *third*
ketika *when*
khas *typical, specialty (of)*
khawatir *worry*
khitanan *circumcision ceremony*
khusus *special, exclusive, particular*
kira-kira *roughly, at a guess*
kiri *left*
kita *we/us/our* (inclusive)
kode pos *postcode*
kolam *pool, pond*
kolega *colleague*
koneksi *connection*

konfirmasi	*confirmation*
koper	*suitcase*
kopi	*coffee*
kosong	*zero, empty*
kota	*town, city*
kredit	*credit*
krupuk	*cracker*
kue	*cake*
kuku	*nail* (body part)
kukus	*to steam*
kuli	*unskilled laborer*
kulit	*skin*
kuning	*yellow*
kurang	*not quite, less, minus*
kursi roda	*wheelchair*
lagi	*again, more*
lahir	*to be born*
laki-laki	*man, male*
lalu	*past, then*
lama	*old, of long duration*
lampu	*lamp*
lampu merah	*red light,* (coll.) *traffic light*
lantai	*floor, level*
lapar	*hungry*
laut	*sea*
lebih	*more*
leher	*neck*
lengan	*arm*
letoi	*tired*
lewat	*past*
licin	*slippery*
lift	*elevator/lift*
lihat	*see, look at*
lima	*five*
loket	*ticket booth*
lontong	*steamed rice cake*
losmen	*guesthouse*
LSM	*NGO*
luar	*outside*
luka	*wound, cut, injury*
lupa	*forget*
lurus	*straight*
lusa	*day after tomorrow*
lutut	*knee*
Maaf.	*Sorry.*
mahal	*expensive*
makan	*eat*
makan malam	*dinner, eat dinner*
makan pagi	*breakfast, eat breakfast*
makan siang	*lunch, eat lunch*
makanan	*food*
makan-makan	*eating (for pleasure)*
mal	*mall*
malam	*evening, night*
mana	*where*
manajer	*manager*
mandi	*bathe, shower* (v.)
mangga	*mango*
mangkok	*bowl*
manis	*sweet*
Maret	*March*
Mari	*Let's, Come*
masak	*cook* (v.)
masakan	*cuisine, cooking* (n.)
masih	*still*
masjid	*mosque*
masuk	*enter*
mau	*want*
Mei	*May*
meja	*desk, table*
meja	*table*
melati	*jasmine*
Melayu	*Malay*
melukis	*paint* (v.)
membaca	*reading*
memberikan	*give (something)*
memesan	*book* (v.), *order* (v.)
menari	*dance* (v.)
mendaki	*climb* (v.)
mendengarkan	*listen to*
menderita	*suffer*
meneliti	*research* (v.)
menelpon	*call* (v.), *ring* (v.)

mengajar	*teach*
mengeja	*spell* (v.)
mengerti	*understand*
menginap	*stay (overnight)*
menikah	*be/get married*
menit	*minute*
menonton	*watch* (v.)
menyeberang	*cross* (v.)
menyenangkan	*pleases, pleasing* (v., adj.)
merah	*red*
mereka	*they, them, their*
merepotkan	*imposing on, overburdening*
merica	*pepper*
mineral	*mineral*
minggu	*week*
Minggu	*Sunday*
minta	*request, ask for*
minum	*drink* (v.)
minuman	*drink* (n.)
minum-minum	*drinking (alcoholic beverages)*
mobil	*car*
muda	*young*
muka	*face*
mulai	*to start*
mulut	*mouth*
muntah	*to vomit*
murah	*cheap*
musik	*music*
naik	*get on, ascend,* (coll.) *ride/take*
nama	*name*
nanti	*later*
negara	*state, country*
nenek	*grandmother*
nganga	*gaping, wide open*
ngantuk	*sleepy*
ngeri	*scary*
nol	*zero*
nomor	*number*
November	*November*
numpang tanya ...	*may I ask ...*
nyala	*ablaze, lit*
nyamuk	*mosquito*
obat	*medicine, drug*
ojek	*motorcycle service*
Oktober	*October*
oleh	*by*
oleh-oleh	*souvenir*
om	*uncle*
operasi	*operation*
orang	*person* (people classifier)
orang tua	*parents*
oranye	*orange*
pacar	*girlfriend, boyfriend*
pada	*at, on, in*
pagi	*morning*
pahit	*bitter*
pakai	*wear, use*
pakaian	*clothing*
paling	*most*
paman	*uncle*
pamit	*part* (v.)
panas	*hot*
pancuran mandi	*shower* (n.)
panggang	*to roast/grill*
panggil	*to call (by name)*
panjang	*long*
pantai	*beach*
papan	*board*
paramedis	*paramedic*
parkir	*to park*
pas	*to fit, accurate, exactly*
pasang	*pair*
pasangan	*partner*
pasar	*market*
pasien	*patient*
paspor	*passport*
pasta gigi	*toothpaste*
patah tulang	*bone fracture*
pedas	*spicy*
pegawai	*worker, employee*
pegawai negeri	*civil servant*

pekerja	*worker*	pesan (n.)	*message*
pekerjaan	*job, occupation*	pesan (v.)	*order*
pekerjaan rumah	*homework*	pesanan	*order* (n.)
pelajar	*student*	pesawat terbang	*airplane*
pelan	*slow*	peta	*map*
pelan-pelan	*slowly*	pinggang	*waist*
pelukis	*painter*	pinggul	*hip*
pembantu	*helper*	pipi	*cheek*
pembuat	*maker*	piring	*plate*
pemesanan	*reservation*	pisang	*banana, plantain*
pena	*pen*	pisau	*knife*
penari	*dancer*	ponsel	*cell phone*
pencak silat	*Indonesian martial arts*	potong	*slice* (v., n.), *cut* (v., n.)
pendek	*short*	praktik	*(medical) practice, to practice (medicine)*
peneliti	*researcher*	pukul	*strike* (v.), *hour* (fig.)
pengajar	*educator*	pulang	*return home*
pengering	*dryer*	pulau	*island*
penginapan	*commercially run accommodation*	puluh	*tens digit*
penjual	*vendor, seller*	punggung	*back* (body part)
penumpang	*passenger*	punya	*have, possess, own*
penyeberangan	*crossing* (n.)	pusat perbelanjaan	*shopping center*
per malam	*per night*	pusing	*light-headed*
perahu	*boat*	puskesmas	*public clinic*
perak	*silver*	putih	*white*
perawat	*nurse*	Rabu	*Wednesday*
perempatan	*intersection, crossroads*	radio	*radio*
perempuan	*woman, female*	ramah	*friendly*
pergelangan kaki	*ankle*	rambut	*hair*
pergelangan tangan	*wrist*	ranjang	*bed*
pergi	*go* (v.)	ranjang bayi	*baby cot*
periksa	*to examine*	rasa (n.)	*flavor, taste, feel*
perjalanan	*trip, journey*	rasa (v.)	*sense, feel*
perlu	*need*	ratus	*hundred*
permisi	*excuse me/us*	rawat	*nurse* (v.), *care for* (v.)
pernah	*ever*	rawat inap	*inpatient care*
persimpangan	*intersection*	rawat jalan	*outpatient care*
pertama	*first, firstly*	rebus	*to boil*
pertigaan	*T-junction*	renang	*swim* (v.)
perusahaan	*company, corporation*	repot	*busy, overburdened*
perut	*stomach*	resep obat	*prescription*
		resepsionis	*receptionist*

reservasi	*reservation*	sebuah	*one thing* (classifier)
restoran	*restaurant*	sedang	*currently*
ribu	*thousand*	sedotan	*straw*
rok	*skirt*	sehari-hari	*everyday* (adj.)
rokok	*cigarette*	sehat	*healthy*
ronsen	*x-ray*	sejak	*since*
roti	*bread*	sekali	*once, one time*
ruko	*shophouse*	sekali (adv.)	*very*
rumah	*house, home*	sekarang	*now*
rumah kos	*boarding house*	sekolah	*school*
rumah makan	*eatery, restaurant*	selalu	*always*
rumah sakit	*hospital*	selama	*for a duration of*
rumah tangga	*household*	Selamat datang!	*Welcome!*
rusa	*deer*	Selamat jalan	*Have a good journey!*
Sabtu	*Saturday*	Selamat malam!	*Good evening/night!*
sagu	*sago*	Selamat pagi!	*Good morning!*
saja	*merely, only*	Selamat siang!	*Good day!*
sakit	*be ill, be sick, ache, hurt, pain*	Selamat sore!	*Good afternoon!*
		Selamat tinggal	*Goodbye!*
salah	*incorrect, wrong*	Selandia Baru	*New Zealand*
Salam	*Regards*	Selasa	*Tuesday*
Sama-sama.	*Likewise., You're welcome.*	selesai	*to be finished, to be done*
sambal	*chili sauce*	seluler	*cellular*
sampai	*arrive, until*	semalam	*a night*
sampaikan	*pass (something) on*	sembarangan	*carelessly*
samping	*side*	sembilan	*nine*
sana	*over there*	sembuh	*recover, get well again*
sandal	*sandal*	semoga	*hope that*
santan	*coconut milk*	semua	*all*
saos	*sauce*	senang	*enjoy, to be pleased*
sapi	*cow*	sendiri	*oneself*
sate	*meat skewer*	sendok garpu	*cutlery*
satu	*one*	seni	*craft, art*
saudara	*relative, sibling*	Senin	*Monday*
saya	*I, me, my*	sentuh	*contact* (n.), *touch* (n.)
sayur	*vegetable*	seorang	*one person* (classifier)
sebaiknya	*it is best that ...*	sepak bola	*soccer*
sebelah	*side*	sepasang	*a pair of*
sebelas	*eleven*	sepatu	*shoe*
sebelum	*before*	sepeda	*bicycle*
sebentar	*a moment*	sepeda motor	*motorcycle*
seberang	*other side*	seperempat	*a quarter*

September	*September*	takut	*afraid of, nervous about*
sepuluh	*ten*	tamu	*guest*
sepupu	*cousin*	tanah	*ground*
sering	*often*	tangan	*hand*
sesudah	*after*	tangga	*staircase*
setengah	*half*	tanggal	*(calendar) date*
setiap	*every*	tanpa	*without, lacking*
setrika	*iron* (appliance)	tante	*aunt*
sewa	*rent* (v.)	tanya	*ask, enquire*
sewaktu	*while*	tarif	*rate, fee, fare*
siang	*daytime (11 a.m.–3 p.m.)*	tas	*bag*
siapa	*who*	tawar	*plain, unsweetened*
sibuk	*busy*	tebus	*to redeem*
sikat	*brush*	teh	*tea*
siku	*elbow*	telepon, telpon	*phone*
silakan	*please, go ahead*	televisi	*television*
singa	*lion*	telinga	*ear*
Singapura	*Singapore*	telur	*egg*
singkong	*cassava*	teman	*friend*
sini	*here*	tempat	*place, location*
situ	*there*	tempat tidur	*bed*
Skotlandia	*Scotland*	tempe	*fermented soy bean cake*
sombong	*snobbish*	tengah	*center, middle*
sop	*soup*	tenggorokan	*throat*
sore	*afternoon*	tentu	*of course*
stasiun	*station*	terakhir	*last, finally*
suami	*husband*	teras	*porch*
sudah	*already*	terbuka	*opened*
suka	*like* (v.)	Terima kasih.	*Thank you.*
sumpit	*chopsticks*	terlalu	*too, overly*
Suster	*Sister*	terlambat	*slow, late*
susu	*milk*	termasuk	*included*
swalayan	*self-service*	tersebut	*mentioned, said*
swasta	*private* (non-governmental)	tersesat	*to be lost*
syair	*poem*	terus	*(continue) onwards*
syal	*shawl*	tetangga	*neighbor*
syukuran	*thanksgiving*	tetapi	*but*
tadi	*earlier*	tidak	*no, not*
tahu (v.)	*know, be aware (of)*	Tidak ada apa-apa.	*Nothing's the matter.*
tahu (n.)	*tofu*	Tidak apa-apa.	*It's nothing., No worries.*
tahun	*year*	tidak enak badan	*unwell*
taksi	*taxi*		

tidak pernah	*never*
tidak usah	*no need to*
tidur	*sleep* (v.)
tiga	*three*
tiket	*ticket*
timur	*east*
tinggal	*live, reside, remain*
tinggi	*tall*
titip	*entrust, leave (something with someone)*
toko	*store*
topi	*hat*
toserba	*department store*
tradisional	*traditional*
trotoar	*sidewalk*
tua	*old*
tugu	*monument*
tujuh	*seven*
tukang	*skilled laborer, handyperson*
tumis	*to stir-fry*
tunggu	*wait*
turun	*get off, descend*
uang	*money (also notes and coins)*
uang kembalian	*change*
uang tunai	*cash*
udang	*prawn, shrimp*
ukuran	*size*
ulang	*repeat*
ulang tahun	*birthday*
umur	*age*
Unit Gawat Darurat	*Emergency Unit*
ungu	*purple*
universitas	*university*
untuk	*for, for the purpose of*
vegan	*vegan*
vegetarian	*vegetarian*
vespa	*scooter*
Wah	(expression of awe)
wajan	*wok*
waktu	*time* (n.)
Wales	*Wales*
warna	*color*
warnet	*internet café*
wartawan	*journalist*
warung	*street stall*
ya	*yes*
yang	*that, which, that which*
Yang mana?	*Which one/ones?*
Yth.	*Dear* (form of address)

English–Indonesian glossary

If an Indonesian word has been presented in more than one form in the book, you'll find both forms listed under the same entry. For example, when you look up the word *work*, you'll find both **kerja** and **bekerja**.

(expression of awe)	*Wah*
(interrogative in yes/no questions)	*Apakah*
(phone greeting)	*halo*
ablaze	*nyala*
able to	*bisa*
above	*atas*
accident	*kecelakaan*
accommodation	*akomodasi*
(commercially run) accommodation	*penginapan*
accountant	*akuntan*
accurate	*pas*
ache	*sakit*
acquaint (someone)	*kenalkan*
acquaintance	*kenalan*
activity	*kegiatan*
address	*alamat*
adopted child	*anak angkat*
advert	*iklan*
airplane	*pesawat terbang*
afraid (of)	*takut*
after	*sesudah*
afternoon	*sore*
again	*lagi*
age	*umur*
aged	*berumur*
ahead	*depan*
airport	*bandar udara, bandara*
alcohol	*alkohol*
all	*semua*
All right.	*Baiklah.*
allergy	*alergi*
alley	*gang*
allowed	*boleh*
already	*sudah*
also	*juga*
always	*selalu*
ambulance	*ambulans*
amenity	*fasilitas*
America	*Amerika*
and	*dan*
ankle	*pergelangan kaki*
antibiotic	*antibiotik*
antiseptic	*antiseptik*
appointment	*janji* (coll.)
April	*April*
Arab	*Arab*
archipelago	*kepulauan*
arm	*lengan*
arrive	*datang, sampai*
art	*seni*
ascend	*naik*
ask	*tanya*
assist (v.)	*bantu, membantu*
at (loc.)	*di*
at (time period)	*pada*
at a guess	*kira-kira*
August	*Agustus*
aunt	*bibi, tante*

Australia *Australia*
available *ada*
avocado *alpukat*
aware (of) *tahu*
baby *bayi*
baby cot *ranjang bayi*
back (body part) *punggung*
back (loc.) *belakang*
badminton *bulu tangkis*
bag *tas*
bamboo musical instrument *angklung*
banana *pisang*
bank *bank*
bathe *mandi*
bathroom *kamar mandi*
bathtub *bak mandi*
battery *baterai*
be cared for *dirawat*
be nursed *dirawat*
be on vacation *berlibur*
be operated on *dioperasi*
be put on an IV drip *diinfus*
be treated as an inpatient *dirawat inap*
be treated as an outpatient *dirawat jalan*
be x-rayed *dironsen*
be/become neighbors *bertetangga*
beach *pantai*
bean *kacang*
because *karena*
become acquainted *berkenalan*
bed *tempat tidur, ranjang*
bedsit *kamar kos*
beef *daging sapi*
beer *bir*
before *sebelum*
below *bawah*
between *antara*
beware (of) *awas*
bicycle *sepeda*
bill *bon*
bird *burung*
birthday *ulang tahun*
bitter *pahit*
black *hitam*
blazer *jas*
blue *biru*
board *papan*
boarding house *rumah kos*
boat *perahu*
body *badan*
boil (v.) *rebus*
bone fracture *patah tulang*
book *buku*
book (v.) *memesan*
born *lahir*
bottle *botol*
bowl *mangkok*
boyfriend *pacar*
bread *roti*
breakfast *makan pagi*
bridge *jembatan*
brown *cokelat*
brush *sikat*
bus *bus, bis* (coll.)
bus stop *halte bus*
busy *sibuk, repot*
but *tetapi*
buy *beli*
by *oleh*
cake *kue*
call (by name) *panggil*
call (v.) *menelpon*
can (v.) *bisa*
Canada *Kanada*
car *mobil*
card *kartu*
care for (v.) *rawat, merawat*
careful *hati-hati*
carefully *hati-hati*
carelessly *sembarangan*
carry *bawa*

cash	*uang tunai*	company	*perusahaan*
cashier	*kasir*	confirmation	*konfirmasi*
cassava	*singkong*	connection	*koneksi*
cell phone	*ponsel*	contact	*hubungi* (vt.), *sentuh* (n.)
cellular	*seluler*		
center	*tengah*	continuing	*terus*
change	*uang kembalian*	converse	*bicara*
change (v.)	*ganti*	cook (v.)	*masak, memasak*
cheap	*murah*		
check	*bon*	cooking (n.)	*masakan*
cheek	*pipi*	corn	*jagung*
cheese	*keju*	corporation	*perusahaan*
chess	*catur*	correct	*betul*
chest	*dada*	country	*negara*
chicken	*ayam*	cousin	*sepupu*
child	*anak*	cow	*sapi*
chili sauce	*sambal*	crab	*kepiting*
China	*Cina*	cracker	*krupuk*
chopsticks	*sumpit*	craft	*seni*
church	*gereja*	craftsperson	*tukang*
cigarette	*rokok*	create (for)	*buatkan*
cinema	*bioskop*	credit	*kredit*
circumcision ceremony	*khitanan*	cross (v.)	*menyeberang*
		crossing (n.)	*penyeberangan*
citrus	*jeruk*	crossroads	*perempatan*
city	*kota*	cuisine	*masakan*
civil servant	*pegawai negeri*	cup	*cangkir*
clear (v.)	*(coll.) angkat*	currently	*sedang*
climb (v.)	*mendaki*	curry	*kare*
clock	*jam*	cut (n.)	*luka*
cloth	*kain*	cut (v., n.)	*potong*
clothing	*baju, pakaian*	cutlery	*sendok garpu*
coconut	*kelapa*	dance (v.)	*menari*
coconut milk	*santan*	dancer	*penari*
coffee	*kopi*	date (calendar)	*tanggal*
cold	*dingin*	day	*hari*
colleague	*kolega*	day after tomorrow	*lusa*
color	*warna*	daytime (11a.m.–3p.m.)	*siang*
come	*datang*	Dear (form of address)	*Yth.*
come (from)	*berasal*	December	*Desember*
Come ...	*Mari*	deer	*rusa*
Come on!	*Ayo!*	delicious	*enak*
Come!	*Ayo!*	dentist	*dokter gigi*

depart	*berangkat*
department store	*toserba*
descend	*turun*
desk	*meja*
destination	*jurusan*
dinner	*makan malam*
(water) dipper	*gayung*
discount	*diskon*
do (something)	*melakukan*
do not (imperative)	*jangan*
doctor	*dokter*
done	*selesai*
double room	*kamar dobel*
downstairs	*bawah* (coll.)
drink	*minuman*
drink (v.)	*minum*
drinking (alcoholic beverages)	*minum-minum*
drug	*obat*
drum and percussion ensemble	*gamelan*
dryer	*pengering*
duck (n.)	*bebek*
ear	*telinga*
earlier	*tadi*
early	*cepat*
east	*timur*
eat	*makan*
eat breakfast	*makan pagi*
eat dinner	*makan malam*
eat lunch	*makan siang*
eatery	*rumah makan*
eating (for pleasure)	*makan-makan*
educator	*pengajar*
egg	*telur*
eight	*delapan*
elbow	*siku*
electronic	*elektronik*
elevator	*lift*
eleven	*sebelas*
embassy	*kedutaan*
Emergency Unit	*Unit Gawat Darurat*
employee	*pekerja, karyawan, pegawai*
empty	*kosong*
end (n.)	*akhir*
engineer	*insinyur*
England	*Inggris*
enjoy	*senang, gemar*
enquire	*tanya*
enter	*masuk*
escalator	*eskalator*
escort	*antar*
Europe	*Eropa*
evening	*malam*
ever	*pernah*
every	*setiap*
everyday (adj.)	*sehari-hari*
exactly	*pas*
examine	*periksa*
exclusive	*khusus*
excuse me/us	*permisi*
exit (v.)	*keluar*
expensive	*mahal*
extra	*ekstra*
face	*muka*
facility	*fasilitas*
fall (down)	*jatuh*
family	*keluarga*
far	*jauh*
fare	*tarif*
father	*ayah, bapak*
February	*Februari*
fee	*tarif*
feel (n.)	*rasa*
feel (v.)	*rasa, merasa*
female	*perempuan*
fermented soy bean cake	*tempe*
ferry	*feri*
fetch	*ambilkan*
few	*sedikit*
finally	*terakhir*
finger	*jari*
finished	*selesai*

fire	*api*
first	*pertama*
firstly	*pertama*
fish	*ikan*
fit (v.)	*pas*
five	*lima*
flavor (n.)	*rasa*
floor	*lantai*
flu	*flu*
follow	*ikut*
following (adj.)	*berikut*
food	*makanan*
for	*untuk*
for (a duration of)	*selama*
for sale	*dijual*
for (the purpose of)	*untuk*
forbidden	*dilarang*
foreign	*asing*
forget	*lupa*
four	*empat*
be free	*bebas*
free	*gratis*
Friday	*Jum'at*
friend	*teman*
friendly	*ramah*
from	*dari*
front	*depan*
fruit	*buah*
fry (v.)	*goreng*
full (as in *sated*)	*kenyang*
garden	*halaman*
general practitioner	*dokter umum*
get off	*turun*
get on	*naik*
get well again	*sembuh*
ginger	*jahe*
girlfriend	*pacar*
give (something)	*memberikan*
glass	*gelas*
go (v.)	*pergi*
go ahead	*silakan*
goat	*kambing*
going to	*akan*
gold	*emas*
good	*bagus, baik*
Good afternoon!	*Selamat sore!*
Good day!	*Selamat siang!*
Good evening/night!	*Selamat malam!*
Good morning!	*Selamat pagi!*
goodbye	*dah*
Goodbye! (when leaving)	*Selamat tinggal!*
goods	*barang*
grandchild	*cucu*
grandfather	*kakek*
grandmother	*nenek*
gray	*abu-abu*
green	*hijau*
ground	*tanah*
guest	*tamu*
guesthouse	*losmen*
hair	*rambut*
half	*setengah*
hand	*tangan*
hand phone	*HP*
handyperson	*tukang*
has/have	*ada*
hat	*topi*
have	*punya*
have ... eyes	*bermata*
Have a good journey!	*Selamat jalan!*
have an accident	*kecelakaan* (coll.)
have an allergy	*beralergi, punya alergi*
he	*dia, beliau* (formal)
head	*kepala*
heading (for)	*jurusan*
health	*kesehatan*
healthy	*sehat*
hear	*dengar*
heart	*jantung,* (fig.) *hati*
hello	*halo*
help (n.)	*bantuan*
help (v.)	*bantu, membantu*
helper	*pembantu*
her	*dia, beliau* (formal)

here	*sini*
him	*dia, beliau* (formal)
hip	*pinggul*
his	*dia, beliau* (formal)
home	*rumah*
homework	*pekerjaan rumah*
homemaker	*ibu rumah tangga*
hope that	*semoga*
hospital	*rumah sakit*
hot	*panas*
hotel	*hotel*
hour	*jam*
hour (fig.)	*pukul*
house	*rumah*
household	*rumah tangga*
housewife	*ibu rumah tangga*
how	*bagaimana*
How are you?	*Apa kabar?*
how many	*berapa*
how would it be if	*bagaimana kalau*
hundred	*ratus*
hungry	*lapar*
hurt	*sakit*
husband	*suami*
I	*aku* (informal), *saya* (formal)
ice	*es*
if	*kalau*
ill	*sakit*
imposing on	*merepotkan*
in (fig.)	*dalam*
in (loc.)	*di*
in (time period)	*pada*
included	*termasuk*
incorrect	*salah*
India	*India*
influenza	*flu*
injury	*luka*
inpatient care	*rawat inap*
inside	*dalam*
internet café	*warnet*
intersection	*persimpangan, perempatan*

intravenous (IV) therapy	*infus*
Ireland	*Irlandia*
iron (appliance)	*setrika*
island	*pulau*
it is best that ...	*sebaiknya*
It's nothing.	*Tidak apa-apa.*
itch (v., n.)	*gatal*
January	*Januari*
Japan	*Jepang*
jasmine	*melati*
Java	*Jawa*
job	*pekerjaan*
journalist	*wartawan*
journey	*perjalanan*
juice	*jus*
July	*Juli*
June	*Juni*
just	*baru* (adv.)
kangaroo	*kanguru*
kitchen	*dapur*
knee	*lutut*
knife	*pisau*
know	*tahu*
know (someone)	*kenal*
laborer (skilled)	*tukang*
laborer (unskilled)	*kuli*
lacking	*tanpa*
lamb	*daging anak domba*
lake	*danau*
lamp	*lampu*
language	*bahasa*
large	*besar*
last	*terakhir*
late	*terlambat*
later	*nanti*
leave (something with someone)	*titip*
left	*kiri*
leg	*kaki*
less	*kurang*
Let me introduce you.	*Kenalkan.*

Let's	*Mari*	may I ask ...	*numpang tanya ...*
level	*lantai*	me	*aku* (informal), *saya* (formal)
life	*hidup*		
lift (up)	*angkat*	meaning	*arti*
light-headed	*pusing*	meat	*daging*
like (v.)	*suka*	meat skewer	*sate*
like that	*begitu*	medicine	*obat*
like this	*begini*	meet	*bertemu*
Likewise.	*Sama-sama.*	mentioned (adj.)	*tersebut*
limit	*batas*	merely	*saja*
lion	*singa*	message (n.)	*pesan*
lip(s)	*bibir*	method	*cara*
listen to	*mendengarkan*	middle	*tengah*
lit	*nyala*	midwife	*bidan*
a little	*sedikit*	milk	*susu*
live (v.)	*tinggal*	million	*juta*
liver	*hati*	mineral	*mineral*
location	*tempat*	minus	*kurang*
long	*panjang*	minute	*menit*
long duration (of)	*lama*	(a) moment	*sebentar*
look at	*lihat*	Monday	*Senin*
look for	*cari, mencari*	money (*also* notes *and* coins)	*uang*
lost (v.)	*tersesat*		
luggage	*bagasi*	month	*bulan*
lunch (n., v.)	*makan siang*	monument	*tugu*
Madam	*Ibu*	more	*lagi, lebih*
make	*buat*	morning	*pagi*
maker	*pembuat*	mosque	*masjid*
Malay	*Melayu*	mosquito	*nyamuk*
male	*laki-laki*	most	*paling*
mall	*mal*	mother	*ibu*
man	*laki-laki*	motorcycle	*sepeda motor*
manager	*manajer*	motorcycle service	*ojek*
mango	*mangga*	mountain	*gunung*
many	*banyak*	mouth	*mulut*
map	*peta*	movie	*film*
March	*Maret*	Mrs	*Ibu*
market	*pasar*	Ms	*Ibu*
married (be/get)	*menikah*	much	*banyak*
martial arts (Indonesian)	*pencak silat*	music	*musik*
		must	*harus*
May	*Mei*	my	*aku* (informal), *saya* (formal)
may	*boleh*		

nail (body part)	*kuku*	Okay.	*Baiklah.*
name	*nama*	old	*tua*
near	*dekat*	old (of long duration)	*lama*
neck	*leher*	on (loc.)	*di*
need	*perlu*	on (time period)	*pada*
neighbor	*tetangga*	once	*sekali*
nephew	*keponakan laki-laki*	one	*satu*
		one time/occasion	*sekali*
nervous (about)	*takut*	oneself	*sendiri*
never	*tidak pernah*	only	*saja, hanya*
new	*baru*	(continue) onwards	*terus*
New Zealand	*Selandia Baru*	opened	*terbuka*
newly	*baru*	operation	*operasi*
news	*kabar*	or	*atau*
next	*berikut*	orange (the color)	*oranye*
NGO	*LSM*	orange	*jeruk*
niece	*keponakan perempuan*	order (n.)	*pesanan*
		order (v.)	*pesan, memesan*
night	*malam*	origin	*asal*
a night	*semalam*	originate from	*berasal*
nine	*sembilan*	other side	*seberang*
no	*bukan, tidak*	our	*kami, kita*
no need to	*tidak usah*	outpatient care	*rawat jalan*
No worries.	*Tidak apa-apa.*	outside	*luar*
nose	*hidung*	overburdened	*repot*
not	*bukan, tidak*	overburdening	*merepotkan*
not quite	*kurang*	overly	*terlalu*
not yet	*belum*	own (v.)	*punya*
Nothing's the matter.	*Tidak ada apa-apa.*	pediatrician	*dokter anak*
		page	*halaman*
November	*November*	pain	*sakit*
now	*sekarang*	paint (v.)	*melukis*
number	*nomor*	painter	*pelukis*
nurse	*perawat*	pair	*pasang*
nurse (v.)	*rawat, merawat*	(a) pair of	*sepasang*
nut	*kacang*	parents	*orang tua*
object	*barang*	park (v.)	*parkir*
(number of) occasions	*kali*	part (v.)	*pamit*
occupation	*pekerjaan*	particular	*khusus*
October	*Oktober*	partner	*pasangan*
of course	*tentu*	pass (something) on	*sampaikan*
office	*kantor*	passenger	*penumpang*
often	*sering*	passport	*paspor*

past	*lalu, lewat*
patient	*pasien*
pay (v.)	*bayar*
pea	*kacang*
peanut	*kacang tanah*
pen	*pena*
pepper	*merica*
per night	*per malam*
person	*orang*
pharmacy	*apotek*
phone	*telepon, telpon, telefon*
photocopy	*fotokopi*
pig	*babi*
place	*tempat*
plain	*tawar*
plantain	*pisang*
plate	*piring*
play (v.)	*bermain, main*
please	*silakan*
pleased	*senang*
please (v.)	*menyenangkan*
pleasing (adj.)	*menyenangkan*
plump	*gemuk*
poem	*syair*
police station	*kantor polisi*
pond	*kolam*
pool	*kolam*
Poor thing!	*Kasihan!*
porch	*teras*
pork	*daging babi*
porridge	*bubur*
possess	*punya*
post office	*kantor pos*
postcode	*kode pos*
potato	*kentang*
(medical) practice (v., n.)	*praktik*
prawn	*udang*
pregnant	*hamil*
prescription	*resep obat*
present (somewhere)	*ada*
price	*harga*
private (non-governmental)	*swasta*
public clinic	*puskesmas*
public transport	*kendaraan umum*
purple	*ungu*
(a) quarter	*seperempat*
quick	*cepat*
quickly	*cepat-cepat*
radio	*radio*
rarely	*jarang*
rate	*tarif*
reading	*membaca*
recently	*baru*
receptionist	*resepsionis*
recognize	*kenal*
recover	*sembuh*
red	*merah*
red light	*lampu merah*
redeem	*tebus*
Regards	*Salam*
relative	*saudara*
remain	*tinggal*
rent (v.)	*sewa, menyewa*
repeat	*ulang*
request, ask for	*minta*
research (v.)	*meneliti*
researcher	*peneliti*
reservation	*pemesanan, reservasi*
reside	*tinggal*
restaurant	*restoran, rumah makan*
return (v.)	*kembali*
return home	*pulang*
ride	(coll.) *naik*
right	*kanan*
ring (v.)	*menelpon*
road	*jalan*
roast/grill (v.)	*panggang, bakar*
roughly	*kira-kira*
roundabout	*bundaran*
safe (n.)	*brankas*
sago	*sagu*

said (adj.)	*tersebut*
salt	*garam*
salty	*asin*
sandal	*sendal*
Saturday	*Sabtu*
sauce	*saos*
say (v.)	*berkata,* (coll.) *bilang*
scary	*ngeri*
school	*sekolah*
scientist	*ilmuwan*
scooter	*vespa*
Scotland	*Skotlandia*
scuba diving	*berselam skuba*
sea	*laut*
search for	*cari, mencari*
second	*kedua*
see	*lihat*
self-service	*swalayan*
sell	*jual*
seller	*penjual*
sense (v.)	*rasa, merasa*
September	*September*
seven	*tujuh*
shall	*akan*
shawl	*syal*
she	*dia, beliau* (formal)
sheep	*domba*
ship	*kapal*
shirt	*kemeja*
shoe	*sepatu*
shop (v.)	*belanja, berbelanja*
shophouse	*ruko*
shopping (n.)	*belanjaan*
shopping center	*pusat perbelanjaan*
short	*pendek*
shorts	*celana pendek*
shoulder	*bahu*
shower (n.)	*pancuran mandi*
shower (v.)	*mandi*
shrimp	*udang*
sibling	*saudara*
sibling (older)	*kakak*
sibling (younger)	*adik*
sick	*sakit*
side	*samping, sebelah*
sidewalk	*trotoar*
silver	*perak*
since	*sejak*
Singapore	*Singapura*
single room	*kamar singel*
Sir, Mr	*Bapak*
Sister	*Suster*
sit	*duduk*
six	*enam*
size	*ukuran*
skin	*kulit*
skirt	*rok*
sleep (v.)	*tidur*
sleepy	*ngantuk*
slice (v., n.)	*potong*
slippery	*licin*
slow	*pelan*
slowly	*pelan-pelan*
small	*kecil*
snobbish	*sombong*
so	*jadi*
soccer	*sepak bola*
socks	*kaos kaki*
sometimes	*kadang-kadang*
Sorry.	*Maaf.*
soup	*sop*
sour	*asam*
souvenir	*oleh-oleh*
soy	*kedelai*
soy sauce	*kecap*
speak	*bicara*
special	*khusus*
specialty (of)	*khas*
spell (v.)	*mengeja*
spicy	*pedas*
spinach	*bayam*
sponge (cake)	*bolu*
spy	*mata-mata*

square (loc.)	*alun-alun*	tens digit	*puluh*
staircase	*tangga*	than	*daripada*
star-rated	*berbintang*	Thank you.	*Terima kasih.*
start (v.)	*mulai*	thanksgiving	*syukuran*
state	*negara*	that	*itu, yang*
station	*stasiun*	that which	*yang*
stay (overnight)	*menginap*	their	*mereka*
steam (v.)	*kukus*	them	*mereka*
steamed rice cake	*lontong*	then	*lalu, kemudian*
stepchild	*anak tiri*	there	*situ*
still	*masih*	(over) there	*sana*
stir-fry (v., n.)	*tumis*	there is/are	*ada*
stomach	*perut*	therefore	*jadi*
stop (v.)	*berhenti*	they	*mereka*
store (n.)	*toko*	thing	*barang*
story	*cerita*	third	*ketiga*
straight	*lurus*	thirsty	*haus*
straw	*sedotan*	this	*ini*
street	*jalan*	thousand	*ribu*
street stall	*warung*	three	*tiga*
strike (v.)	*pukul*	throat	*tenggorokan*
student	*pelajar*	thumb	*ibu jari*
study (v.)	*belajar*	Thursday	*Kamis*
suffer	*menderita*	thus	*jadi*
suitcase	*koper*	ticket	*karcis*
Sunday	*Minggu*	Ticket booth	*loket*
surfing	*berselancar*	ticket booth	*loket*
sweet	*manis*	tie	*dasi*
swim (v.)	*renang, berenang*	till	(coll.) *kasir*
switch (v.)	*ganti*	time (n.)	*waktu*
table	*meja*	(number of) times	*kali*
take (away)	*bawa*	letoi	*tired*
take (transportation)	*naik* (coll.)	T-junction	*pertigaan*
take (v.)	*ambil*	to	*ke*
taken home	*dibawa pulang*	to (someone)	*kepada*
tall	*tinggi*	today	*hari ini*
taste (n.)	*rasa*	toe	*jari kaki*
taxi	*taksi*	tofu	*tahu* (n.)
tea	*teh*	together	*bersama*
teach	*mengajar*	toilet	*WC, toilet,* (fig.) *kamar kecil*
-teen	*belas*		
television	*televisi*	tomorrow	*besok*
ten	*sepuluh*	too (also)	*juga*

too (overly)	*terlalu*
tooth	*gigi*
toothpaste	*pasta gigi*
touch (n.)	*sentuh*
town	*kota*
traditional	*tradisional*
traffic light	*lampu merah* (coll.)
train (n.)	*kereta api*
train (v.)	*berlatih*
travel on foot	*jalan kaki*
trip (n.)	*perjalanan*
trousers	*celana panjang*
try (v.)	*coba*
T-shirt	*kaos*
Tuesday	*Selasa*
turn (v.)	*belok*
two	*dua*
typical	*khas*
uncle	*om, paman*
underclothes	*baju dalam*
underground	*bawah tanah*
understand	*mengerti*
university	*universitas*
unsweetened	*tawar*
until	*sampai*
unwell	*tidak enak badan*
upstairs	*(coll.) atas*
us	*kami, kita*
USA	*Amerika Serikat*
use (v.)	*pakai*
usually	*biasanya*
vegan	*vegan*
vegetarian	*vegetarian*
vegetable	*sayur*
vehicle	*kendaraan*
vendor	*penjual*
very	*sekali (adv.)*
village	*desa, kampung*
vomit (v.)	*muntah*
waist	*pinggang*
wait	*tunggu*
Wales	*Wales*
walk (v.)	*jalan, jalan kaki*
walking about	*berjalan-jalan*
want	*mau, ingin*
warm	*hangat*
watch (v.)	*menonton*
water	*air*
way	*jalan*
we	*kami, kita*
wear (v.)	*pakai*
Wednesday	*Rabu*
week	*minggu*
Welcome!	*Selamat datang!*
well	*baik*
well done	*bagus*
west	*barat*
what	*apa*
What a pity!	*Kasihan!*
what about	(coll.) *bagaimana kalau*
What's the matter?	*Ada apa?*
wheelchair	*kursi roda*
when	*ketika, kalau*
When (interrogative)	*Kapan*
where	*mana*
whether	*apakah*
which	*yang*
Which one/ones?	*Yang mana?*
while	*sewaktu*
white	*putih*
who	*siapa*
why	*kenapa*
wife	*istri*
will	*akan*
wish (v.)	*ingin*
with	*dengan*
(along) with	*bersama*
within	*dalam*
without	*tanpa*
wok	*wajan*
woman	*perempuan*

work (v.)	*kerja, bekerja*
worker	*pekerja, karyawan, pegawai*
worry	*khawatir*
wound	*luka*
wrap (v.)	*bungkus*
wrapped	*dibungkus*
wrist	*pergelangan tangan*
wrong	*salah*
x-ray	*ronsen*
yard	*halaman*
year	*tahun*
yellow	*kuning*
yes	*ya*
yesterday	*kemarin*
you	*Anda, kamu, kalian* (plural)
You're welcome.	*Sama-sama. Terima kasih kembali.*
young	*muda*
your	*Anda, kamu, kalian* (plural)
zero	*nol, kosong*

Can-do statements

UNIT	CEFR level	ACTFL level	CAN-DO STATEMENTS
UNIT 1	**A1**	**Novice High**	I can introduce myself and others and can ask and answer questions about personal details.
UNIT 2	**A1**	**Novice High**	I can indicate time. I can introduce others. I can ask and answer questions about personal details.
UNIT 3	**A1**	**Novice High**	I can recognize familiar words concerning self and family. I can ask how people are and react to news.
UNIT 4	**A1**	**Novice High**	I can ask and answer questions about personal details. I can handle time.
UNIT 5	**A1**	**Novice High**	I can handle numbers, quantities, and cost. I can ask about things and make simple transactions in stores.
UNIT 6	**A1**	**Novice High**	I can fill in forms of personal details for myself or others. I can explain what I like or dislike.

UNIT	CEFR level	ACTFL level	CAN-DO STATEMENTS
UNIT 7	**A1 / A2**	**Novice High / Intermediate Low**	I can indicate time. **(A1)** I can get simple information about travel, use of public transport, and buy tickets. **(A2)**
UNIT 8	**A2**	**Intermediate Low**	I can understand short, simple texts such as menus. I can make and respond to suggestions.
UNIT 9	**A1 / A2**	**Novice High / Intermediate Low**	I can recognize familiar words concerning concrete surroundings. **(A1)** I can understand everyday signs. **(A2)**
UNIT 10	**A1 / A2**	**Novice High / Intermediate Low**	I can follow short, simple directions. **(A1)** I can describe habits, past activities and personal experiences. **(A2)**